Disclaimer

This eBook is not endorsed by Provo Craft, nor is the author associated with the Provo Craft company or organization in any way. I receive no funding from Provo Craft for this book, nor is there any relationship assumed between myself and the company. This eBook does not in any way promote or suggest sponsorship, connection, license, or association with Provo Craft or Cricut. I am simply a fan and a user myself, and wished to share my knowledge with others based on what I have learned and self-taught myself. Any criticisms, comments, or opinions are that of the author and not the thoughts or ideas of the Provo Craft company in any way, shape or form.

Acknowledgments

To my family, who tolerates my crafting.

Commonly Used Terms

Common Terms, Abbreviations, and Lingo for Cricut Users

Weeding- weeding is the removal of excess materials

HTV- heat transfer vinyl

Oracal- a type of vinyl; comes in permanent and removable

SVG-scalable vector graphics

JPG/JPEG- joint photographic experts group

PNG-portable networks graphics

Heat press- a heat pressing machine used to make t-shirts and other items requiring heat transfer vinyl

Blades- various cutting blades used for the Cricut

Transfer sheets- contact paper or other sticky paper used to transfer vinyl

Scraper- tool used to help with vinyl and cardboard lifting, depending on project

Chapter 1

Welcome to your Cricut!

Welcome to the world of Cricut. So, you've got your machine, and now you're probably asking, "now what?" You may even be too scared to take it out of the box. Have no fear, that's why this book is here! Don't be intimated. This is meant to be a fun item to use and the possibilities are endless as far as what you can do with is amazing machine!

You can do this! There are many options for you as a crafter, and the uses of a Cricut are endless. Whether you are a scrap booker, a hobby vinylist, or a professional small business owner, there are many options available for you for use with your Cricut.

All About Your Machine

The Cricut machine started out for scrapbooking enthusiasts in the early 2000s. They basically simplified things. Now, however, Cricuts are used the world over for many different things such as sign making, making t-shirts, and just about anything else that you can think of in regard to crafting. Cricuts make it super easy to create and craft, so let's start by talking about which version of Cricut YOU might have. Though please remember, this eBook is geared towards those with a Cricut Explore machine.

Various Versions of the Cricut

Cricut has been around since the early 2000s. There are several versions of machines out there, and you want to make sure that you are using the correct one for your needs. Without further ado, let's look at a little bit of the machine history.

Original Cricut

This is the original Cricut machine. This was the original version that came out when Cricut first came out. You can usually find these used for around $25-50. They use cartridges, are not very software supported, and use a 6 x 12" mat. This is a very basic Cricut, but if you don't need something fancy, this machine may work for you. You can use the Cricut Design Craft Room, but the software is not the easiest to use. We will talk about this a bit more later.

Cricut Create

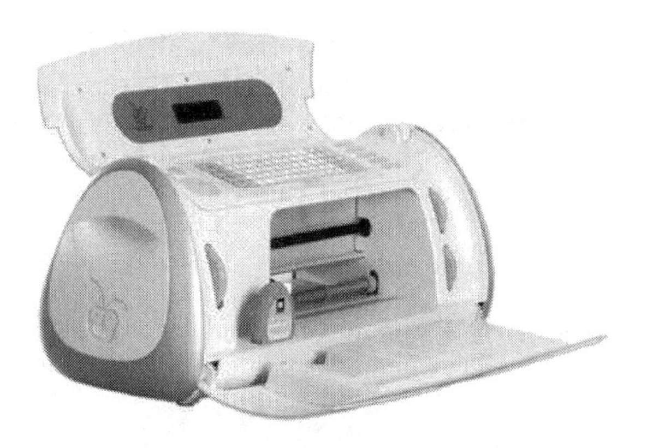

The Create was the next version of the Cricut that was released. Again, this is a 6x12" cutting surface, and uses cartridges versus software. You can usually find these used for about $25-50 if you are wanting to get your feet wet in the Cricut World. You can use the Cricut Design Craft Room, but the software is not the easiest to use.

Cricut Expression

The Expression is the next Cricut in line. This is an upgrade from the Create and Original, as it offers a much larger cutting surface. You can use a wider variety of materials with this machine, and you can also use electronic cutting options. You can also specify better how to cut the material that you are working with. This Cricut works with the Design Craft Room, which we will talk about in a bit. Used, these run around $50-100.

Cricut Cake

The Cricut Cake was put out around the same time as the Expression. The Cake offered a great tool to make specialized cakes using templates and cartridges, as well as special cutting mats and tools. These are no longer supported by Cricut, but you can occasionally find them for sale for around $80 or so. If you are using this for cake, you will need special tools for cutting, and these are difficult to locate. You often need to find 3rd party sellers for these tools. You also need to use special cake cartridges for this Cricut machine.

Expression 2

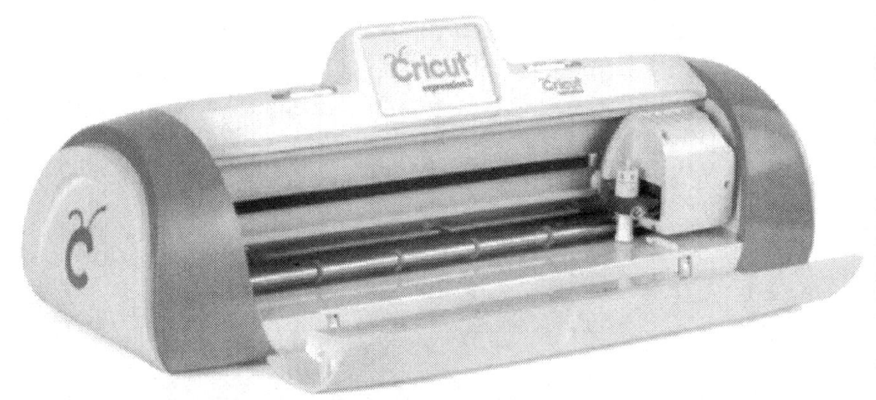

This machine followed the original Expression. This machine did not come with a mat, but had a full on electronic LCD touch screen to operate it. This machine offered image rotation, and again, a larger cutting size. You can still find these machines used for around $50 or so.

Cricut Mini

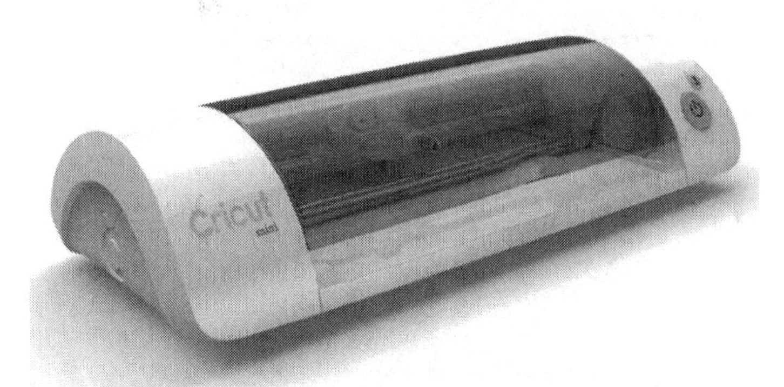

This Cricut only works with a computer, and you use the Cricut Software. You can use a Gypsy (which we will discuss in the accessories chapter!) or you can use the Craft Room Design Software.

Cricut Explore Series

The Explore series is the latest and most up to date Cricuts that are available on the market. Some are being sold right now from $75-250 depending on the store, location, etc. You can find these used, and occasionally they are listed on Craigslist or other yard sale sites, but this is rare. (If you see one, snap it up!)

There are limited differences between the three machines, so we will discuss these. All use the Cricut Design Space software for creation. All of them have various settings and can cut many materials. The Explore One requires that you be hooked to a computer to operate in design space. It is Bluetooth adaptable, and the part for this runs anywhere from $10-50. There is no additional writing tool adapter for the Cricut Explore One. It has a single blade holder. The Explore Air, is Bluetooth adaptable, and comes with an adapter for tools, writing utensils, etchers, etc. And finally, the Explore Air two has everything the Explore Air has, only Cricut claims it is twice as fast. (It can also cost twice as much depending on where you buy your machine from.)

Cricut Explore One

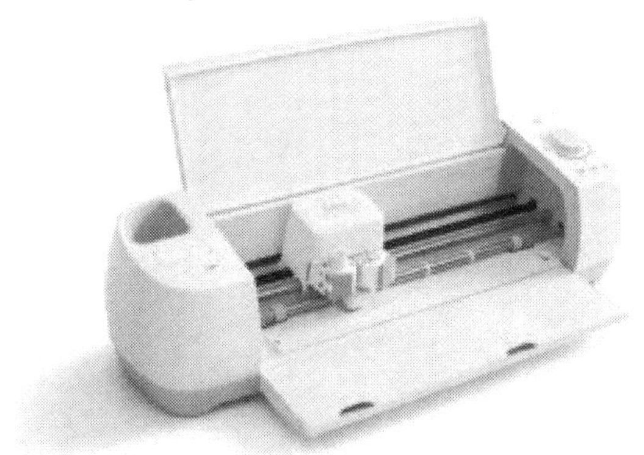

Cricut Explore Air

Cricut Explore Air 2

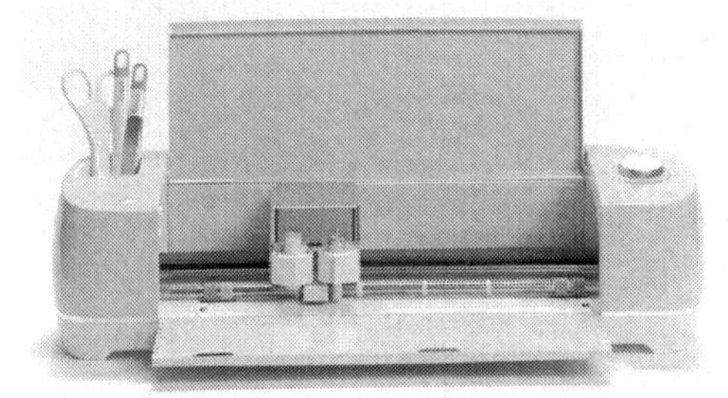

Cricut Maker

Cricut's latest machine, the Cricut Maker, was released on August 20, 2017. Cricut's most recent member to the family boasts of some powerful options. Cricut says this machine will cut fabric and leather, as well as cutting out patterns for sewing. There are some new rotary cutting blades and pens, and you can hookup your tablet to the machine itself. Its price is not cheap, as it runs a $399.00. With that said, it is why this book is primarily covering the Explore machine.

Cricut Parts (Explore, Explore Air, and Explore Air 2)

Ok, so we've now gone through the series of Cricut Machines, let's look at the different parts. For this eBook, we will be using the Explore series of machines, as these are the most up to date and commonly used machines now. (I have taken the liberty of using my own Explore One as the example for this booklet, and have used an iPhone for the photos.)

This is what your machine will look like when it's out of the box and you are ready to turn it on:

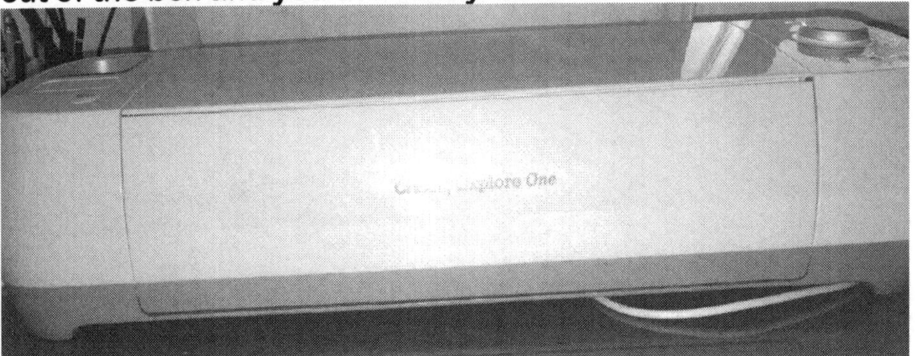

Top left of the machine you have your tool holder, your open button to open the machine, and your slot for inserting cartridges.

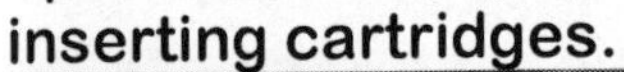

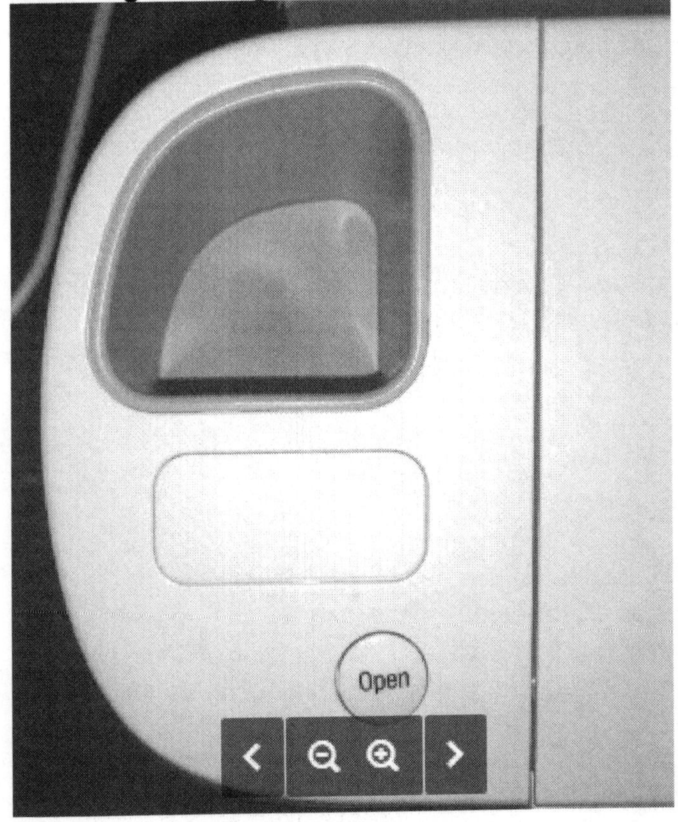

On the left-hand side of the machine, you have your power button, your adjustable material dial, and your feed, cut, and pause buttons. (More about these later, I promise!)

Then we have the open machine with the slot(s) for your cutting blades or writing tools. Note: if this is an Explore Air or Explore Air two, there will be a double slot. The double slot can hold a scoring tool, a pen, or whatever you need in that second holder. The Explore One only has one slot currently that is interchangeable.

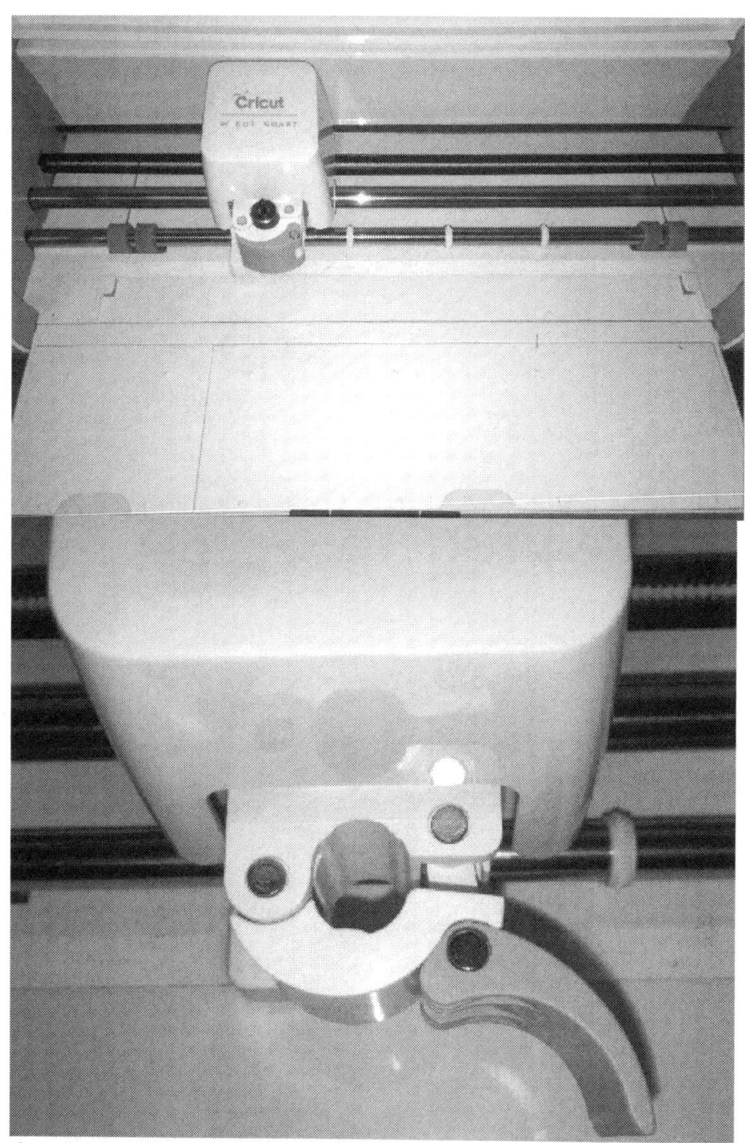

And you have your storage for the smaller supplies such as blades, writing tools, etc.

And finally, in the back you have your power cord adapter plugin in and your USB cord plugin. And that's the machine. It is very easy to use. You simply plug in the USB cord into your computer and the software will begin downloading. Once this is done, you can create your Cricut account and start crafting!

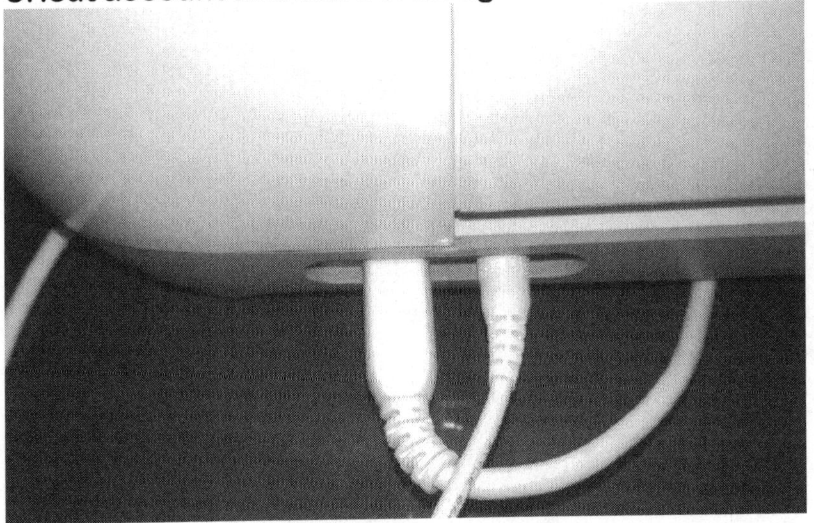

Software for the Cricut

So now comes the next part of the program, and that is all the various types of software that you have no doubt heard about as you have been working with the Cricut. There are several options, and I will briefly discuss those now.

Cricut Cartridges

Cartridges are the first way people are introduced to the Cricut. Back in the "good old days" cartridges were the only way to get the Cricut to work. You would plug in your cartridge, apply the overlay, and enter numbers and codes and manually adjust the Cricut to use the Cartridge you had selected.

There are hundreds of cartridges available, and with that thousands of images available on the cartridge.

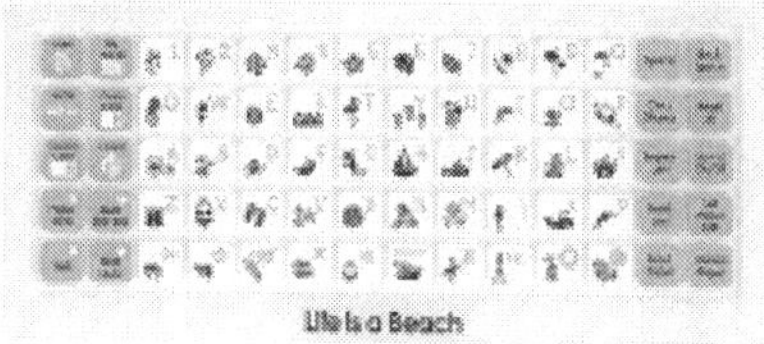

'or sometimes bad) thing about the
ıu can "link" them to your Design
.e software that Cricut uses.) This is
.ad because once you link the cartridge,
ıt electronically; no more plugging it into the
. On the other hand, if you are buying used to get
.ed, you will often find that the cartridges are already
.nked, and you can't use them digitally. Some people buying cartridges online or used get a rude surprise when they find the cartridges are already linked.

At any rate, there are thousands of images available via cartridges. Joann's, Hobby Lobby and craft stores are the best place to purchase the cartridges. They often go on sale from anywhere from $17-50. Cricut even does monthly specials where you can get a couple of free cartridges in a monthly package that they have available, which we can talk about a little later in this book.

Cricut Design Space

Next, we have the Cricut Design Space. Design Space is Cricut's very own software that they have for the Cricut Machine. You access this via the web at https://design.cricut.com/. The software will ask you to login and then you will see the homepage. (You can see via the picture below that I am logged in already.)

Design Space also comes with various subscriptions where you can access nearly all Cricut's images and fonts for a price per month (or per year.) It is up to you to decide if you want to use this. For a beginner, it can be a great tool. For others who like to make or create their own designs, you will find that it may not be worth it to you to utilize the subscription. We will talk more about design space later, and even do a step by step tutorial on how this works. I will also explore other methods of getting graphics, fonts, and how to use these within Design Space.

Design Space is internet based. You need to have an internet connection to be able to use the software itself. This is probably the biggest complaint that Cricut users have- that Design Space requires an internet connection.

This is the newest software that Cricut has released, and it is a big improvement over the previous Design Space that was fraught with errors.

Cricut Craft Room

Cricut Craft Room is software that is used for older machines. It is somewhat limited in what you can do and how you can use it as you cannot bring your own designs to the software itself. Overall for those just getting started with a used machine, it can be a useful tool in the getting started on basic Cricut usage.

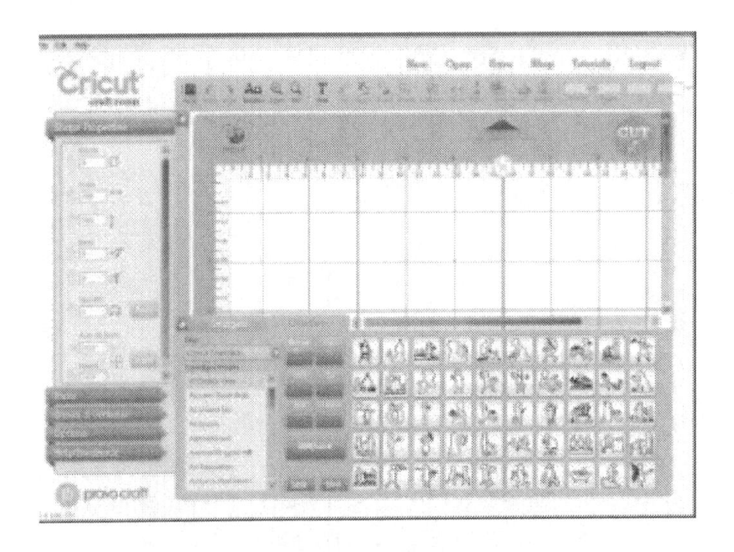

Third Party Software

And then finally, we have some third-party software. In 2010 and 2011 ProvoCraft, the parent company of Cricut, filed lawsuits to stop this. It's their product, and their design, but I believe that this happened because Cricut was mad that someone found a way around their expensive cartridges. At the time, the cartridges were upwards of $50.00. You could not use your own designs or fonts. Software designers found a way to make software available that was compatible, and cartridges were no longer required to be used. The lawsuit was eventually settled, and third-party sellers could no longer link their software for the Cricut. Ultimately the new Design Space has made the reasons for the lawsuits obsolete, as you can use your own fonts and designs now. So, with that said, I will say that third party software is available, but if you use it, you use it at your own risk.

End of Chapter Author's Note

As I am sure you already know, there are tons of how to videos out there online to use your Cricut. I am a visual learner, but I like to have a book handy when I am learning something and to read versus watching someone else do it. That is primarily why I wrote this book. I hope that for those of you that learn by reading can find something solid within its chapters.

This is your basic introduction to the Cricut machines. As posted above you can often find these machines used at garage sales or second-hand stores. Your best bet, however, is to start with one of the newer machines. This will save you in frustration and in time as you will have the most up to date software and tools at your fingertips.

Make sure you have a good solid computer to work with. This is a key ingredient to making sure that your projects run smoothly. A dedicated laptop might even be a good idea if you are in business or want to keep track of just your Cricut stuff. You should also not use Internet Explorer or Edge for a web browser if you can help it. It's not compatible, and it's not the safest choice in browser today.

Chapter 2

Software, Software, Software!

Cricut Cartridges

Everyone is pretty much aware of Cricut Cartridges. These are the original tools to get the machine to work. To use a Cartridge, you plug it into your machine, and follow the steps on the machine. Or, if you are wanting to, you can link a cartridge in Design Studio by doing the followings steps:

1. Visit http://design.cricut.com and sign into your Cricut account
2. Once you log in, click again on the triple line Home button on the far left and select "Cartridge Linking" from the drop-down menu
3. Check to be sure that your Cricut is powered on and is connected to your computer.
4. Insert the cartridge into the Explore port.
5. Once the cartridge is noted to be in the machine, you will be prompted to link the cartridge to your Cricut.com account. Click "Link Cartridge." Once this is done, the cartridge is now linked and cannot be linked to another account.

The cartridge is linked and you can view this within your account. You can pull up the images and fonts to use with any project from here. Make sure to save the box that the cartridge came in. Failure to do so may cause you to lose the cartridge should anything happen to it and the system crash or misplace your files. (And yes, this has happened on occasion.

If you are using an older machine, you will find the booklets and the overlays for the machine itself. There are literally hundreds of cartridges with thousands of images. You can find used and linked cartridges for as little as $5.00 on eBay or garage sale sites if you are looking to just get started. (Remember though- if a cartridge has already been linked, you cannot link it to your Cricut account.)

Every month Cricut also sells various “packages” or “Mystery Boxes” from their website. They usually include one or two cartridges in the packages along with Cricut vinyl, supplies, and other materials.

Cricut Software

We’ve discussed the Design Space a bit already, so just know that this book will cover this version software. Chapter 4 is our step by step instruction chapter, and we will cover the basic need to know info for Design Space. We will explore basic usage of the program and how to manipulate a few things, so if your curiosity is peaked, you can head on down to Chapter 4 to get started. Otherwise, hang tight, and we will introduce the basics and how tos shortly.

iPad/Tablet Versus Computer

Cricut offers Design Space for tablets, phones, and computers. It is my personal recommendation to use a computer, but if you need or want to design on the go, it's nice to have that option too. You can synch your tablet or phone via Bluetooth if your machine is Bluetooth enabled, and you can save the designs that you create to the Design Space save center.

Some people prefer to design using their tablet or phone. It is a personal choice, and it is one you can try out yourself. Look for the "Cricut Design Space" app in your favorite app store.

Off-Brand Software

As I mentioned in Chapter 1, there is third party software. You can still find this available on the web, but you use it at your own risk.

Access Subscription

Cricut offers monthly and yearly subscriptions to their plans that they call "Access Plan." You can use these, or you can upload your own images and fonts (which I'll talk about here shortly.) These "Access Plans" give you access to thousands of images, fonts, and more right from the convenience of the Design Space software program. No need to download or add any additional items into your software; it is all right here and available for you.

Cricut offers three different types of plans:

Membership Plans

The perfect starter package | Amazing value for everyone | The full package!

Currently, as of this writing, the plans are prices as follows:

Monthly cost	$6.99 (billed monthly)	$9.99 (billed monthly)	n/a
Yearly cost	$59.88 (billed annually) Just $4.99/mo. ~ a 29% savings!	$95.88 (billed annually) Just $7.99/mo. ~ a 20% savings!	$119.88 (billed annually) Just $9.99/mo. ~ the best value!
	Sign Me Up	Sign Me Up	Sign Me Up

* 50% off does not include images, fonts, or cartridges from Walt Disney Company® (Disney Consumer Products, Inc.), Sesame Workshop®, Sanrio Hello Kitty®, Boys Scouts of America®, Anna Griffin®, and Lia Griffith® licensors. Discount cannot be combined with other discounts, including Cricut Circle, promotions, and promotion codes and cannot be used on in-app purchases. Cricut reserves the right to add or remove content, and to otherwise modify this offer at any time in the sole discretion of Cricut.

Or if you want to pay monthly for any of these subscriptions they are as follows:

Fonts

You may, however, want to use your own fonts in design studio. This is doable and is welcome in Design Space.

So where can you get additional fonts? Well I will share some of my favorite places with you, as well as how to download and use these fonts.

First up, is DaFont. http://www.dafont.com. There are thousands of fonts available for personal use, commercial use, and to sample. To download a font, you will click on the font "download" button and it will open the file. It will look like this:

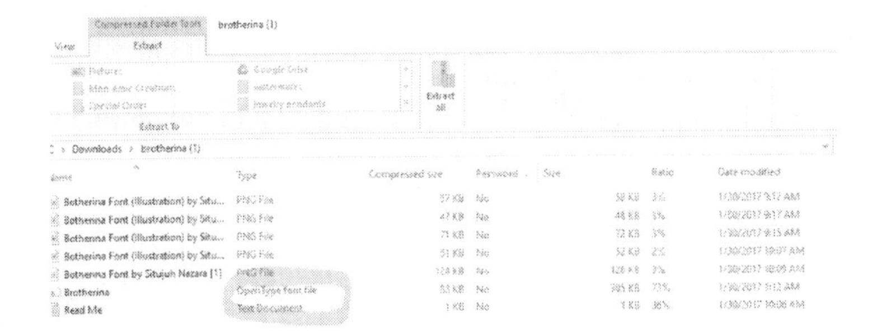

You can "Extract All" or you can double click on the OpenType font file or the True Type file and open the file from here like this:

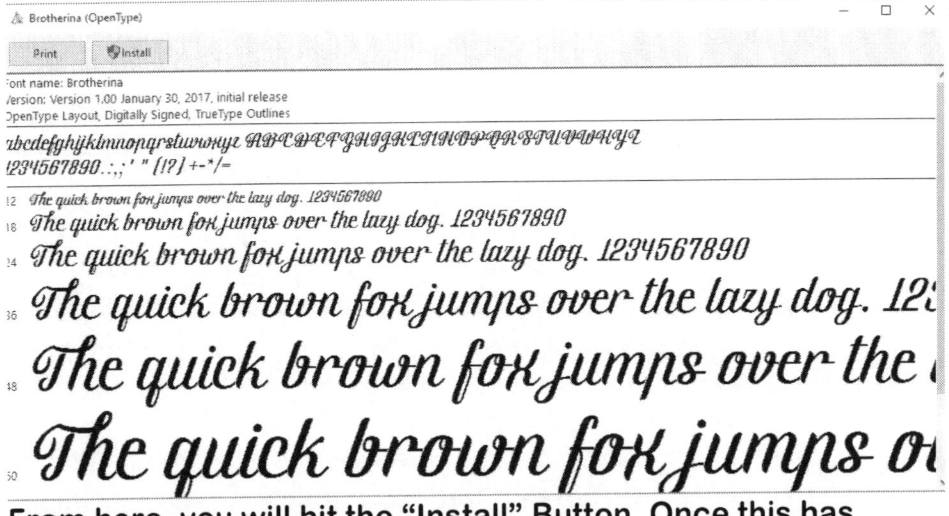

From here, you will hit the "Install" Button. Once this has been installed, it will go "blank" where you can't install it anymore and you can close the windows.

Once you go into Design Space, and view your fonts, it will be loaded in there. You may need to log out and log back in again, but the font will be loaded and available for you to use from there. (And occasionally, you may also need to shut the computer down and turn it back on for the font to register system wide.)

Here is my full list of recommended font websites:
http://www.dafont.com
http://www.thehungryjpeg.com
https://www.fontsquirrel.com/
http://www.1001freefonts.com/
http://www.fontspace.com/
https://www.urbanfonts.com/

And if you ever forget what fonts that you have installed, you can visit http://www.wordmark.it/ and enter a phrase to see your downloaded fonts on your computer! This is also helpful if you are looking to see what fonts look good as well. It's a great tool, and I highly recommend it.

SVG Files Galore

Probably the most commonly asked question is, can I use my own images? Or can I create my own images. Yes, you can! There are a few ways to do this. Cricut primarily uses SVG files or, scalable vector graphics. You can use PNG or JPEG images, but SVGs work the best as they are the most versatile and work the best in Cricut Design Space. (Note: if you are a new Explore owner, your machine comes with FREE designs that are available in the Cricut Access Studio and you can locate them once your machine is set up.)

If you're like me and like to do your own thing you can make your own SVG images in Inkscape. That, however, is a whole other book that I won't be going into today. The software can be found at http://www.inkscape.org. It is not the most user-friendly program, so caveat emptor. There are many tutorials out there on how to use this, and Inkscape has several themselves. I highly recommend using these if you wish to use this software.

Secondly, there are tons and tons of websites, Facebook groups, and various services that offer free SVG files. They are everywhere. A favorite of mine is http://www.openclipart.org. Another great one is http://www.lovesvg.com. The Facebook groups are great for gathering free SVG files.

Note: if you choose to join the Facebook groups, beware of some of their archaic and childish rules. I think some of the people that run these groups are on a power trip and they don't make for a fun time. Moderators tend to ban and delete people without warning. They also may be profiting off you by their "special" status with various companies, and while they offer discounts, make no doubt about it, that they are getting some type of a kickback from the companies that they advertise. Most do not disclose this that I have seen!

You probably want to know: "how do you upload these into your Design Space software?"
First, you'll want to create a new project.

Next, upload images

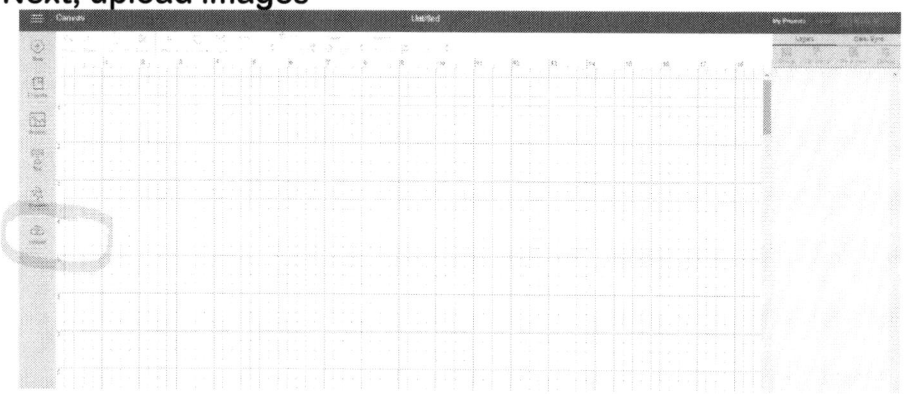

Upload

Cut your images for free (basic and vector).

Images can be .jpg, .gif, .png, .bmp, .svg, or .dxf files

Upload Image

Recently uploaded images View All

Pattern fill

Use your patterns or photos as a fill on any layer

Images can be .jpg, .gif, .png, or .bmp

You will find them in the layer attributes panel under print, then patterns

Upload Pattern

Drag & drop file here

or

Browse

.png, .jpg, .gif, .svg, .dxf, .bmp

Upload image

New

Projects

Images

Text

Shapes

Upload

Cut your images for free (basic and vector)

Images can be .jpg, .gif, .png, .bmp, .svg, or .dx

Upload Image

Recently uploaded images View All

Uploaded

Uploaded

Uploaded

Pattern fill

Use your patterns or photos as a fill on any layer

Images can be .jpg, .gif, .png, or .bmp

ⓘ You will find them in the layer attributes panel under print, then patterns.

Upload Pattern

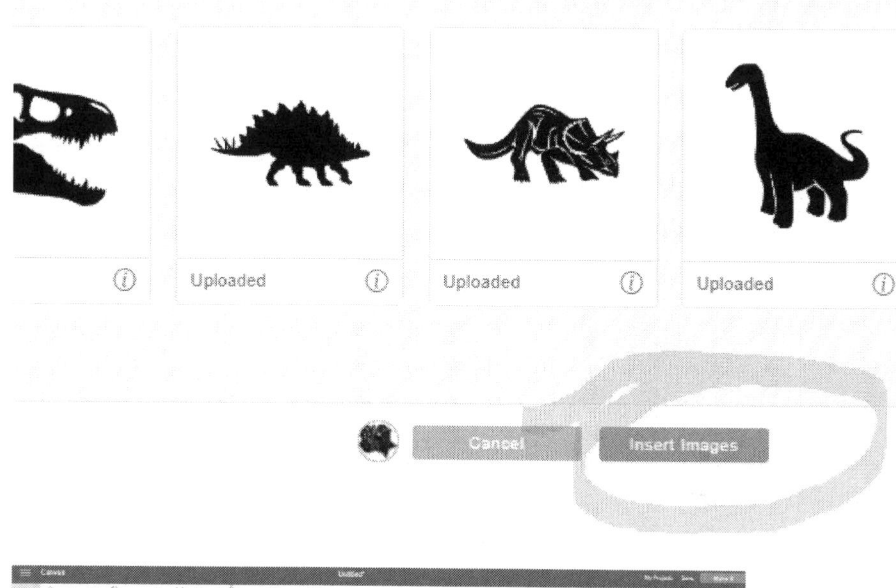

And voila! Your image is now in the Cricut program for you to play with. I recommend going through this step a few times. Particularly if you are new to folder saving. I also recommend saving a specific folder on your desktop to upload with in the beginning until you get more comfortable with this step. It can help save you from pulling out your hair!

Authors Chapter End Note

I have used the Cricut Access, but I also do some graphic design and can make my own images. What you choose to do is up to you, but Design Space does allow for a lot of versatility, and if you want to use your own stuff, you certainly may. If you are going into business, be very careful about the images you use. Some are copyrighted, and if you are caught selling them, you can be on the hook for a lot of money.

As far as the app goes, I have Design Space on my phone and my tablet as well. It's nice when I am sitting waiting for an appointment or waiting to do something and have some downtime and can design. It's not always easy, and sometimes it will hang up, but it is nice to have the option available to save and go back to later.

Chapter 3

Even Machines Need to Accessorize!

In this chapter, we are going to explore anything and everything that you might need to get started using your machine. I will list what you will need and even give some alternatives to where you can buy things that are a bit cheaper than what Cricut charges. Tools and accessories help make your Cricut world turn around!

Blades

First and foremost, you will need blades. I recommend having a few of these to start. It is recommended that you have regular blades and deep cut blades. (Note- you will need a housing tool for the deep cut blade, and this runs right around $20.00.) I recommend looking online to buy your blades. You can certainly get them from Cricut, but you can get German Carbide Blades (6) for around $10.00.

Tip: did you know that you can sharpen your blades by poking them a few times into aluminum foil to extend the life of your blades?

If you are finding that your Cricut is no longer cutting as well, always check and replace the blade- often this is due to some material hanging on the blade, or the blade is getting dull. If material is getting ripped or not cutting, just check the blade!

Cutting Mats

The next thing you will need of course, is a cutting mat. There are a few different options for this that Cricut has available.

Cricut offers several of cutting mats and a couple of different sizes. The purple mat is your strong grip mat and is extra sticky. The green mats are your standard mats and are used for a lot of various materials. The blue mat is the light grip mat, and is often used for delicate materials or cardstock. The pink mat is now available and is primarily for fabric cutting and goes well with the Cricut Maker. It looks like this:

You can order these directly from anywhere Cricut items are sold. Some folks report that if they order them from online at various online stores, they will send them an extra 3-6 packages when they order. I have had this happen a couple of ties, and it is always a pleasant surprise when it happens. I currently have enough to last a year thanks to the generosity of a certain online large retailer.

Keep the mats clean by using the plastic cover that comes with it- they become gunked up easily. They may occasionally need cleaning. My recommendation is to use Awesome Clean from the dollar store. To use, spray it on the mat, let it sit for a minute, scrape the gunk off, and then rinse and dry. Your mat will be good as new.

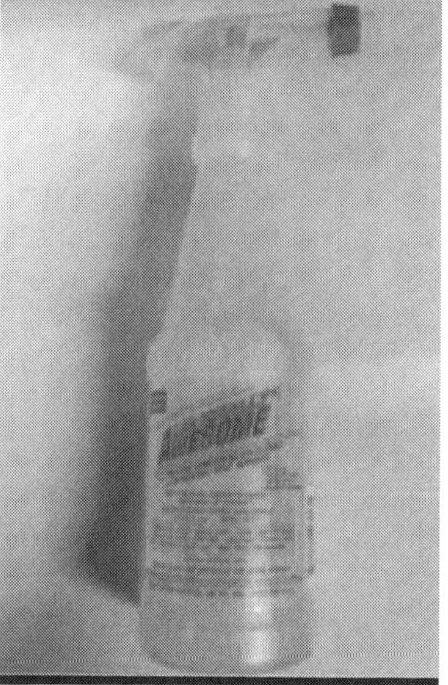

In some cases, though you may need to re-sticky a mat. In that case, I recommend repositionable adhesive spray. To do this, tape the sides of your mat with masking tape and spray an even coverage of the adhesive spray. I personally use Krylon, because it's the best and you can find it at various craft stores relatively cheap.

Now, if you need it, Cricut also offers an extra-long cutting mat that is 12” by 24” for those larger cutting projects. These are hard to find in stores, but you can find them online and at Cricut.com.

Cricut Tools

Cricut sells a tool set for beginners that includes a spatula, scraper/squeegee, weeding hooks, and scissors. This is a great tool set for beginners, and I still have all my original pieces, though I have added others to it as well.

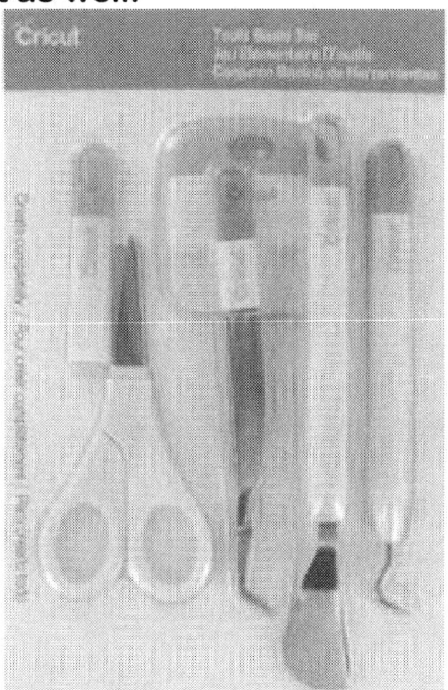

<u>Weeding Tools</u>

If you are getting into vinyl of any kind, you will hear a lot about weeding tools. Cricut provides some good ones, but I also recommend getting a dental pick set as well. This helps to rotate through your various weeding tools, and keeps the picks sharp. You can pick these up at any craft store, or if you know a dentist, just ask for an extra set!

<u>Etchers</u>

Etching with the Cricut is a relatively new concept, and it is something that I am relatively new at as well. Cricut doesn't necessarily make an etching tool itself, so you do have to purchase one third party. Chomas Creations makes a great one that I use myself. It is $30.00 and is available online.

Here is an example of one piece that I have etched so far:

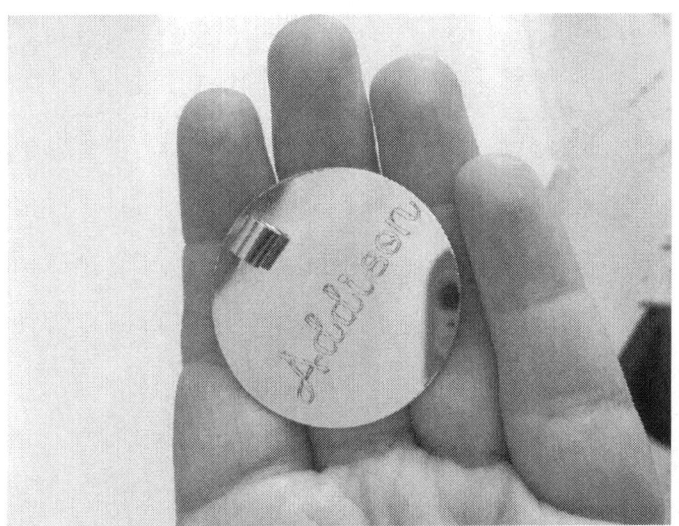

You will need to use etching blanks, as well as customized settings on your Cricut, so this is not a beginner project, but is one that you can get in to as you advance your skills using the Cricut. eBay is one of the best places to locate etching blanks that you can practice with.

Blades

There are many types of blades to use with the machine. They are housed in the cutting unit. There are deep cut and regular cut blades. You can usually buy German Carbide blades that are equivalent on Amazon for a fair price.

The Cricut Maker also offers some various cutting tools such as a rotary cutter for fabric and a different blade housing unit.

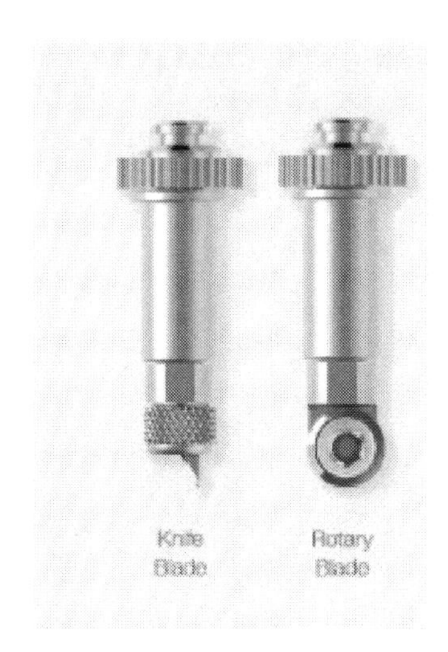

Cartridges

I know I have discussed this already, so I won't beat this horse again. You can get cartridges anywhere Cricut items are sold. You can also find them used and second hand on eBay, online retailers, Craigslist, and other market places. If you want to make sure they are unlinked, you do need to check first, or if you don't care, then purchase away. You can usually find these second hand anywhere from $1-10 depending on the cartridge and where you are buying it.

New cartridges can be found online, and at any place that sells Cricut branded items.

Markers/Writing Utensils

Yes, your Cricut can write. So, you need writing tools. Cricut sells these on their website, and you can also find them at craft supply stores that sell Cricut branded items as well.

You may also use many other marker brands, so long as you have the adapter tool in your Cricut machine. A lot of users swear by the Crayola skinny markers, and have much success using these.

Squeegees/Scrapers

You will need squeegees and scrapers. Cricut sells these and you can find them just about anywhere that sells these. Check your dollar store, supply store, etc. Often you can find them for as little as $0.25. Grab a few and save them because they are easy to lose.

Scoring Tool

For those of you looking to make cards and other items, you will need a scoring tip or a scoring tool to help with this.

You can use a traditional scoring tool like this:

Or you can use the scoring tip blade that will go directly into your housing unit on your Cricut machine.

Cuttlebug

One other cool tool that Cricut makes is the Cuttlebug. This is an embossing machine that you can use with your cards and other items to greatly give it some "flavor."

The Cuttlebug uses die and embossing folders to make patterns, prints, shapes and more. It is another little handy tool, and again there are other options out there, but if you want to stay within the Cricut line, the Cuttlebug is where it's at. There will be no tutorial on this, because embossing is a whole other side of crafting, and it would be another book long.

Gypsy

The Gypsy is a tool that is no longer being manufactured or sold by ProvoCraft, but it is still a tool that occasionally pops up in a few places. You can only use it with the versions prior to the Explore series. This tool allows you to use multiple cartridges at once. You can occasionally find these in second hand stores, at yard sales, and on eBay. They are not sold new anywhere that I know of.

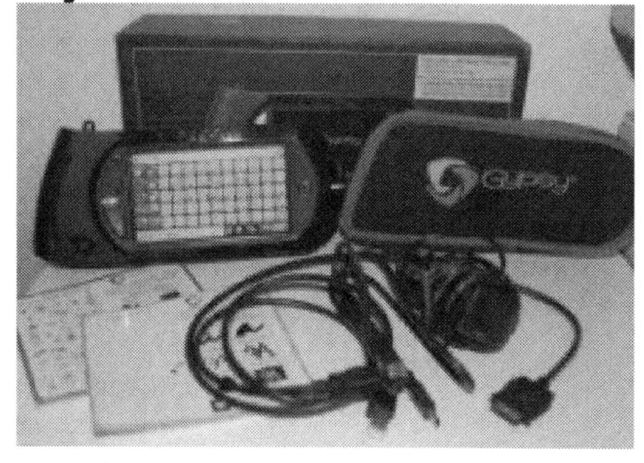

Author's Chapter End Note:

Cricut itself makes some great tools to go with their machines. These are all great for beginners. I think that you will find, however, that you may prefer other brands and other items that suit you as a crafter, and that is perfectly fine. Remember that this should be fun, not frustrating. That means using the tools and items that support your work. You may also be a bit more budget conscious and need to save money. In that case, using off brands may be a requirement, not just a preference.

Chapter 4

Get to Work! A Tutorial in Design Space

Here we go! Do not be afraid to get started with your machine. I see so many people say that they are afraid to even take their machine out of the box. Hang in there! The machine is not smarter than you, and it can't bite you. I promise! There WILL be mistakes- this, I can guarantee. In fact, I have been doing this for quite some time, and I still make mistakes. But as our favorite artist Bob Ross says, "there are no mistakes, just happy accidents!" Jump right on in the water and get your feet wet!

Getting Started

If you haven't already done so, the first thing you are going to want to do is take your machine out of the box and strip off the plastic and wrapping. Look it over. (It sure is pretty! And you may want to decorate it and make it even prettier!) Make sure that everything is accounted for. (It does occasionally happen where someone has opened a "new" box only to find out that it was a return, or a reject, or something is missing.) Now, if you've already done this, you are one step ahead of the game. You will find the power cord and the USB cord. The USB cord will be what you need to set up your account on your computer. Plug everything in and power the machine on.

Next you will want to take a few minutes and go ahead and register your machine. Sometimes, Cricut has thrown in a limited subscription to Design Space for you, so you will want to check for a code for this. It is usually located in the bottom of the box or with the paperwork packet for the Cricut Machine. You can sometimes also find free codes for this online as well.

Make sure your computer is turned on, and then plug in the USB cord into the plug in on your computer. Give it a few minutes to install and recognize the Cricut. Then be sure to visit http://design.cricut.com.

In the upper left-hand corner, there will be a drop-down menu. You will need to select “New Machine Setup.” Here is where (if you don’t already have one) you will create your Cricut account and login, and register your machine. This is also where you will log in to your account later to be able to use the Cricut Design Space software.

Follow the steps, register your account and get ready to get started working in Design Space.

Let’s log in to Design Space together. To star, visit http://design.cricut.com In the upper left-hand side, you’ll see a green “Account” Button. Click on this.

You can choose to always stay logged in, or require a password each time; it is solely your preference.

Signout Successful
You have signed out successfully

Sign In with your Cricut ID
Use your Cricut ID for everything you do with Cricut

Email/Cricut ID

Password

Forgot?

Remember Me

Sign In

Don't have an account yet?

Create A Cricut ID

Once you get to the landing page, in the upper right-hand corner, click on new project:

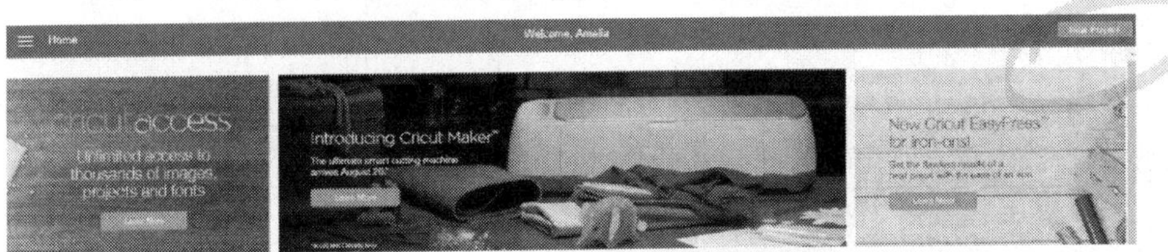

And this is what your blank screens will look like once you are all logged in:

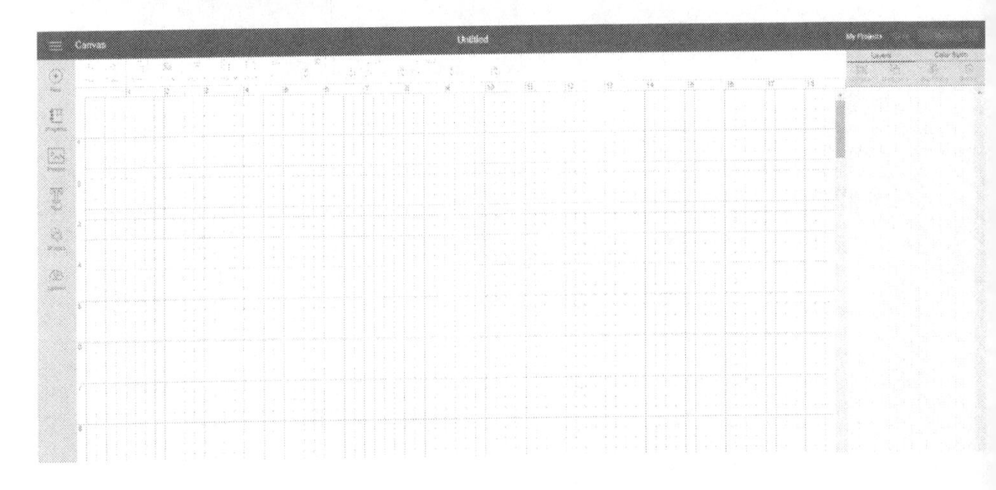

Let's walk through what each item does step by step.

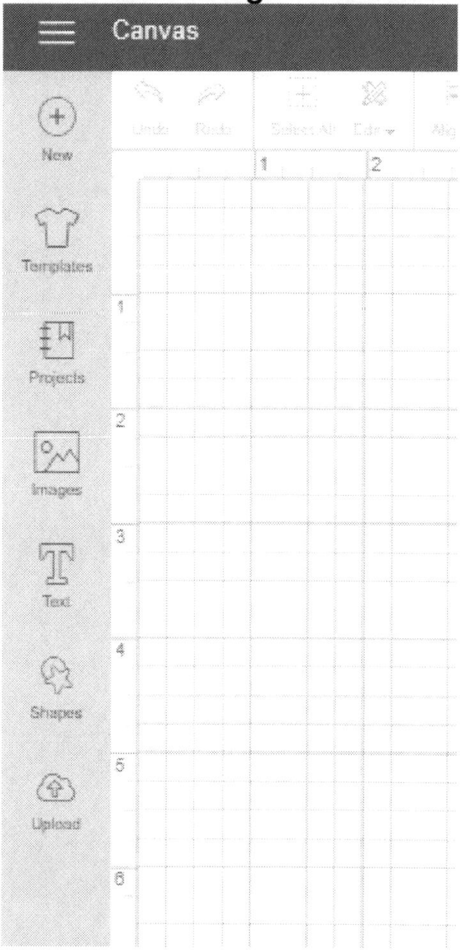

"Templates" allows you to view various templates for your projects. Maybe you are making a t-shirt, or an apron- the template button will allow you to put a template into our project to preview how it will look once finished.

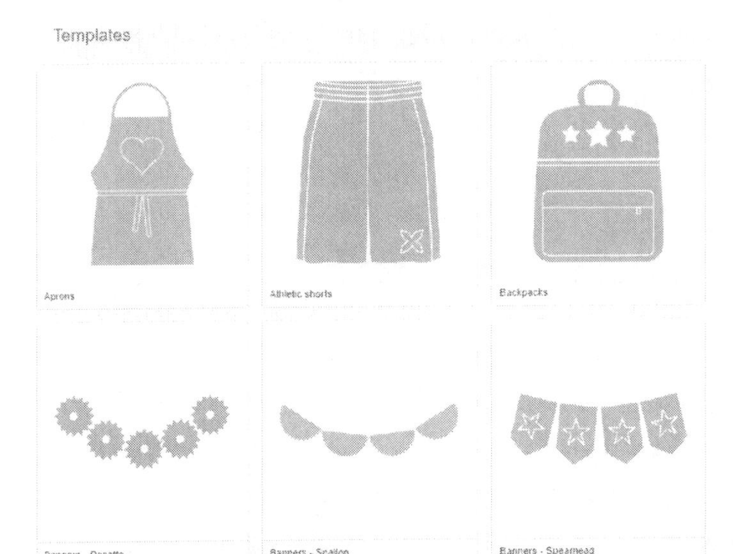

"Projects" is where your saved projects will be located. Anything you have saved you can find in here.

If you click on "Images," this will take you the Access Studio by Cricut.

Click on this and explore what is available. You don't have to have a subscription to view the images, and if you have linked cartridges, this is where you will find them

In the Access studio, you can view various categories and cartridges. You can also search for what you are looking for as well. Let's say you don't have an access subscription, but there is an image that you are after. You can buy the images individually here, and once you purchase them, they are yours to keep.

Images will also show you all the images available in Design Space.

Categories allows you to sort by the categories available. This can include holidays, hobbies, cards, etc.

And finally, cartridges can also show you the cartridges that you have linked to your account.

To go back to your canvas, hit CANCEL in the bottom right of the screen. This will take you back to the blank page in Design Space.

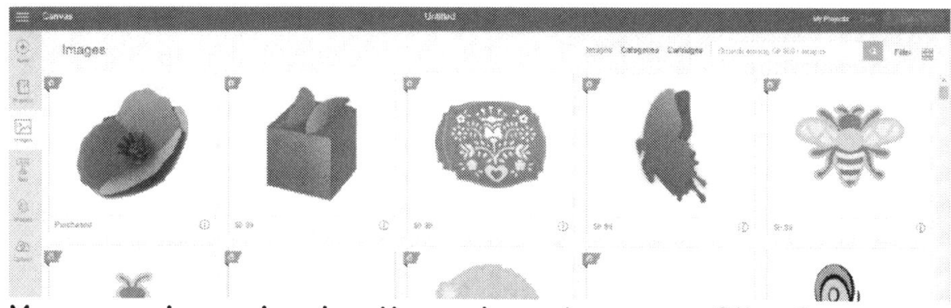

You can also upload patterns here to use as filler for your designs if you plan to make your own designs in Design Space. Hit CANCEL to return to the Design Space canvas.

"Text" will allow you to type your project and select the text size and shape that you wish to use.

"Shapes" will allow you to insert various shapes into the design space project.

"Upload" allows you to upload your own images and ideas into Design Space. This is a great tool if you design your own SVG files.

Make It Now" takes you back to the project screen where Cricut Tutorials will walk you through step by step how to do some of their creations.

New is to make a new project.

My Projects saves your projects, and the Save As allows you to save your projects as you need to, or to change the name of a previously saved project.

Up at the top of the screen you will have your tool bar:

You have all your options to maneuver and change whatever is needed up here. Including font changes, rotating, flipping, etc. Nearly everything you need is up here when it comes to changing the size and shape of whatever it is you are wanting to cut.
On the right-hand side is where you can insert images, insert shapes, and start new projects, so let's play around with that just a little bit.

Let's start here by making a star. In the shapes section, pick a star and make a large star on your "canvas."

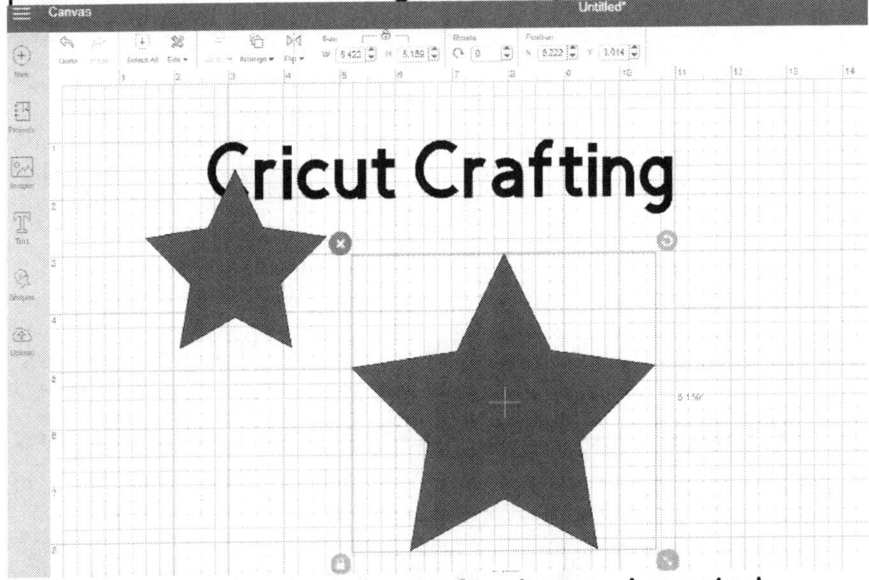

The slice button "slices" out of an image. I created a smaller star, put this over top the larger one, held them both together and then hit slice. It "sliced" out the smaller star, so there is now an empty spot in the middle of the large star. The slice buttons can be found in the lower left-hand corner.

Slice
Weld
Attach
Flatten
Contour

Cricut Crafting

ion molds your images together. I took two together with the shift key, and hit s your images into one another. This can r font as well when you want a font to print or ed together and you want it to stay together. A lot of people forget this step, and therefore your fonts don't want to stay together. Keep this in mind later, and particularly if you are sing a cursive font!

(A welded star.)

The attach option attaches your items together so that when you go to cut your item they will be together. This is particularly helpful when working with font, so that it doesn't get all messed up and ungrouped. We will look at this a little bit more later.

The flatten tool turns your images into single layer images so that you can print and cut with this feature. It also allows separation of layers of various designs into one flattened layer. This is not a tool that I use very often, and it can complicate a design.

And finally, under the layer option, we have the Contour. The contour tool allows you to get rid of unnecessary lines and cut options in your images. Cricut explains how to use this option here:

https://help.cricut.com/help/design-space-contour

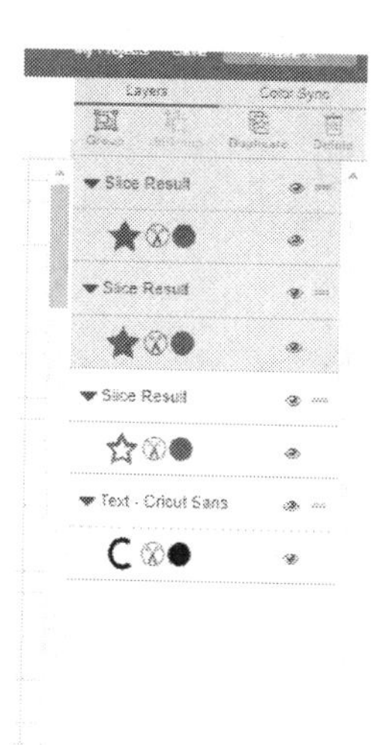

The layers button allows you to view the various layers you are working with. Here you can hide views, remove items, and your slice, weld, attach, flatten, and contour buttons are all at the bottom. You can GROUP your items together to make sure that they print or cut together, and you can change the color of them here as well.

Let's go back to our star for just a moment. Click on it. You will get a box that surrounds the start.

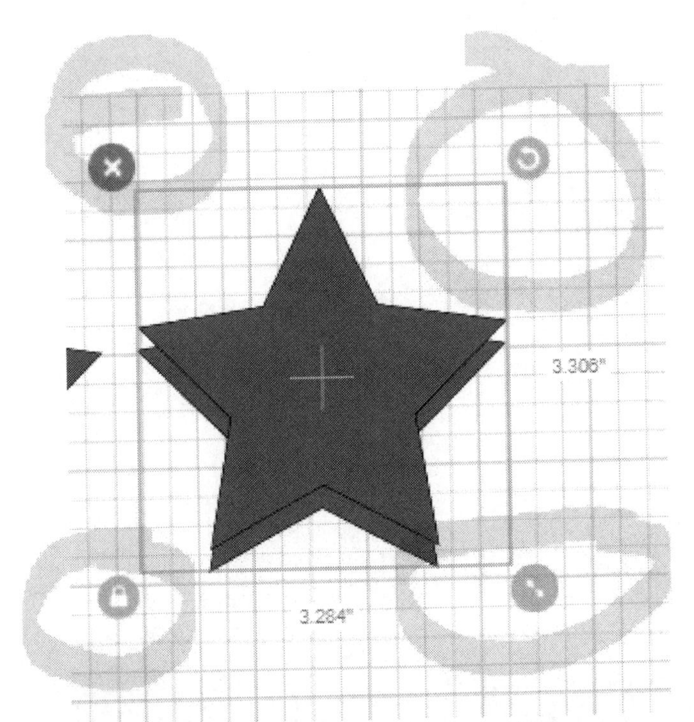

The X will delete the item in question.
The lock if you click on this will allow you to “skew” the design and change its measurements.
The double arrow will allow you to drag and pull to resize.
And finally, the rounded arrow will allow you to change the position of the start by rotating it.

Next, type your name into Design Space.

Cricut Crafting

So, go ahead and highlight the name. Just click on it until a box appears. Now under the edit tab, you will have quite a few more options with editing.

This is where you can change your font, change the text size, rotate the font, etc.
Let's change the font. Click on the "font" tab, and be prepared to wait a bit if you have a lot of fonts installed. And once it loads it will show you all the fonts available, including Design Space fonts from Cricut. Change it to something fun that you like, and change the size of the font.

Let's say though that you only want to see fonts that you own or that you have purchased. How do you do that? Up above the "fonts" you'll see an All Fonts tab; click on this and then select either System Fonts or Cricut Fonts. If you are a fan of a font site and have a lot of personal fonts downloaded, these will show up under System Fonts.

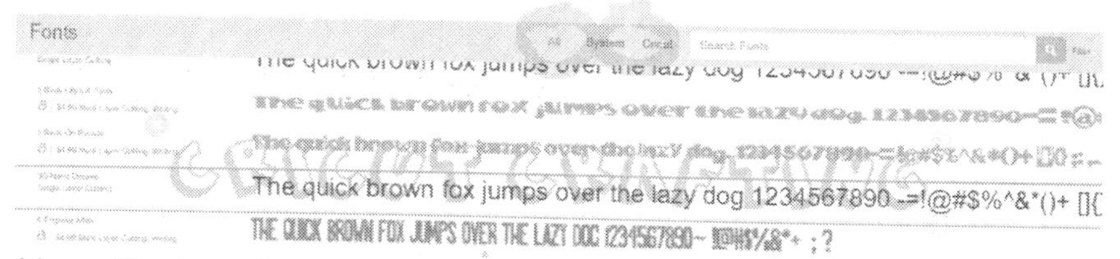

Now that we've entered some font, let's have some fun with the colors.
Let's move back over to the Layer tab.

Click on your name or the word that you chose to use for this exercise. Just make sure the box is around it.
From here, go back over to the menu, and click on the "C" (or the first letter of the word you are using, and you will get this popup menu:

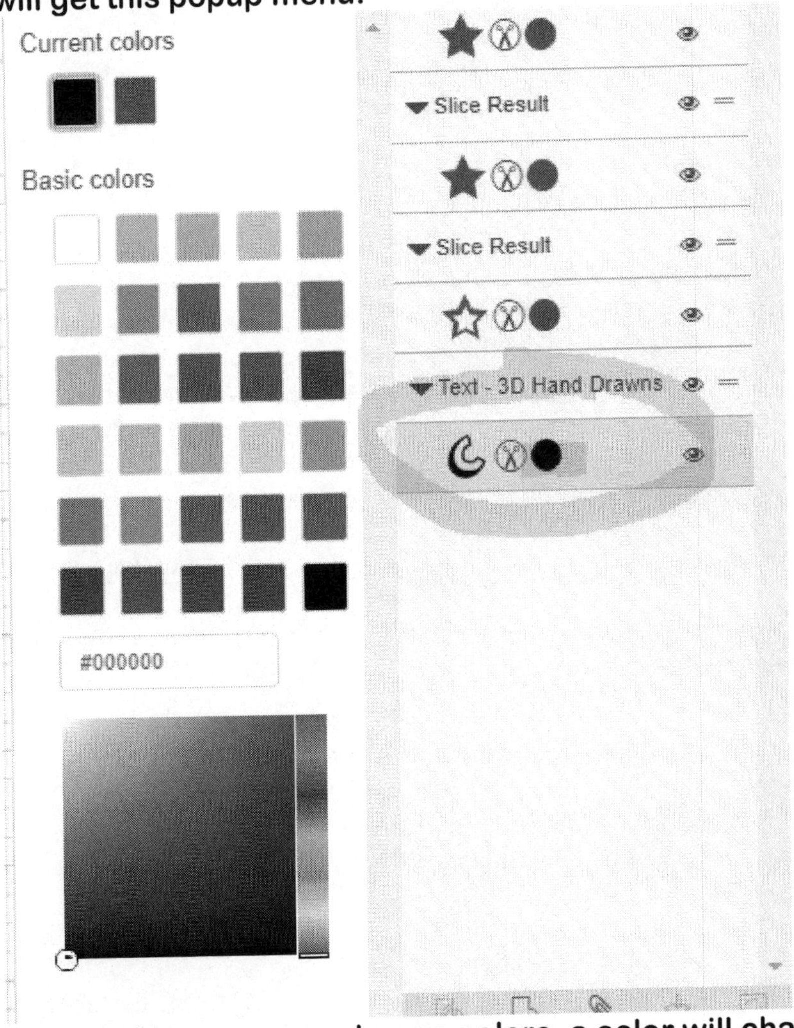

This is where you can change colors, a color will change the font color.
Go ahead and pick a color and the word will change to that new color you have selected.

CRICUT CRAFTING

Now there are also a couple of fun options here. Let's say you want to engrave, or write the wording above, versus printing or cutting it.

Click on the "scissor" icon next to the color dot. You will see now that you can see "Color, Write, Score, and Print" at the top. Click on WRITE.

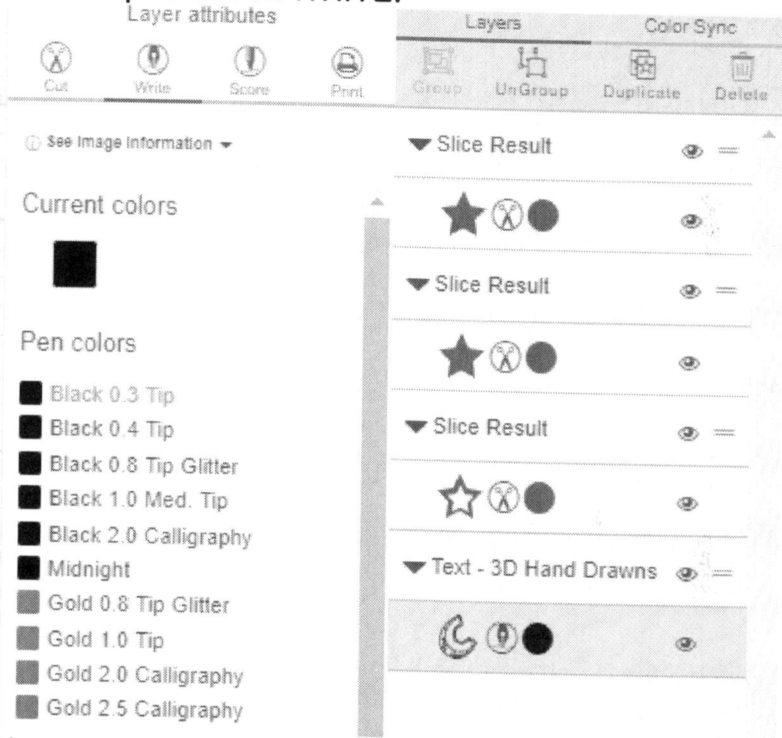

Here you can decide what to "Write" rather than cutting and printing your project. It gives you many options for doing this. It's really a neat tool, and has a lot of options for it.

Scoring is what is used to "Score" a piece of paper usually for folding.

Print is the option you would use for cutting and print. Printing will give you two options. Colors and Patterns.

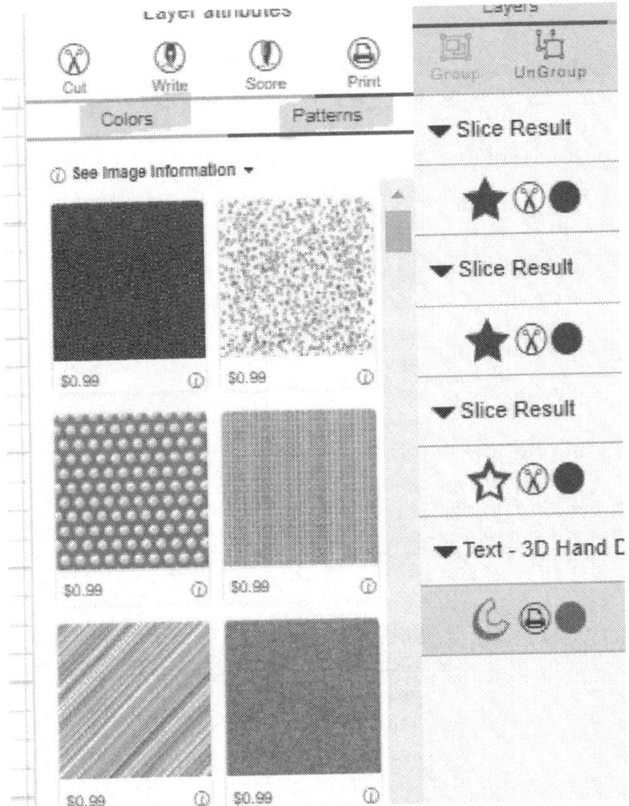

If you are wanting a pattern for your items, this is where you can find them, or you can always upload your own!

For the most part, you will want to stick with Cut and Write for your choices of what to do. If you choose to set your printer up for cut and print, that's great, but that is a more advanced option that I will not be able to cover in this e-book. (There are some great YouTube tutorials that will walk you through this!)

Let's revisit our menu and wrap this up.

The sync button is where you can "sync" your layers up. Let's say you have a few items that are multi-colored, but want them to be almost all the same color. Here is where you can do that, and the sync button will demonstrate how it's done. You basically "drop" the layers onto one another and it will make them the same color. It's simple to do, so feel free to play around with this a few times and get comfortable with it. This will help you save your materials and products so that you are not wasting so much and not overusing.

Now let's complete our first project with some layers and get familiar with a few things.

First, pick out an image that has a few layers in it and upload it into Design Space. I will use one of my own designs that I created.

Here, I have input my image into Design Space.

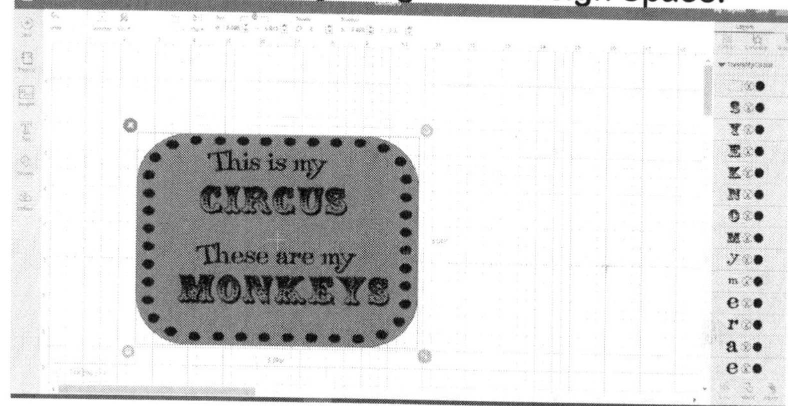

As you can see, this has a couple of different colors and a few different layers.

Let's examine some of the menu items to see what we can see.

First, I want to change the color of the pink. I don't want the image to be pink. I am going to click on the image, and a box will form around the entire image. I am then going to go over to my right-hand side menu, and find my box. I will then click the round color tab next to it and change the color.

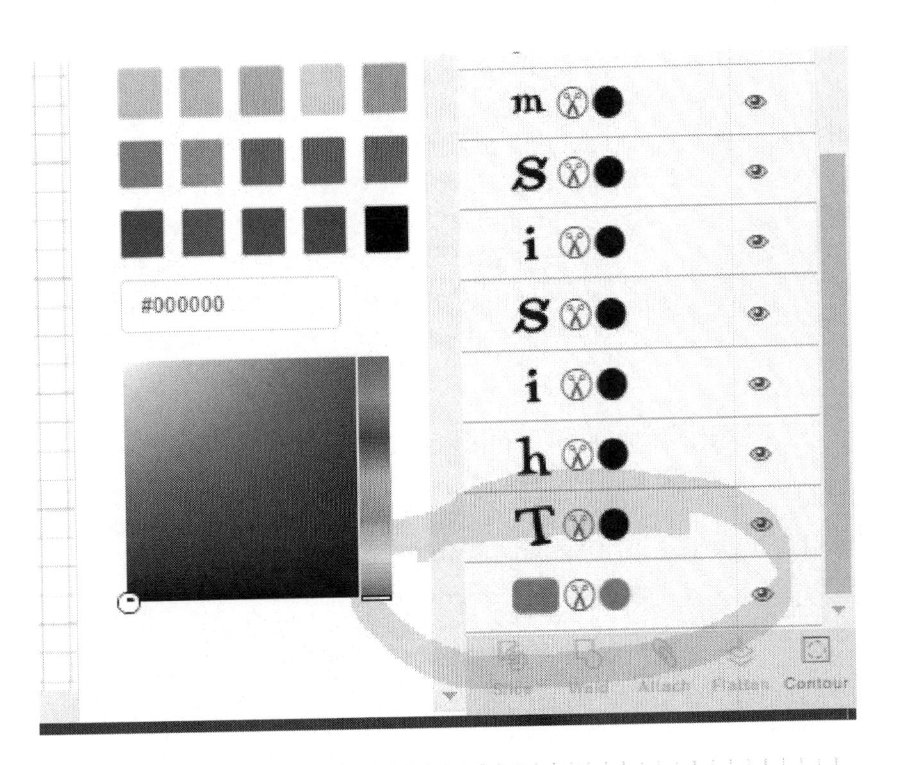
#000000
m
S
i
S
i
h
T
Slice
Weld
Attach
Flatten
Contour

This is my
CIRCUS
These are my
MONKEYS

I want to make sure that when I go to cut and print this, that it will all be attached.

Grab the entire thing, font and all, and select it.

And now we want to attach everything together so that it will all print and cut appropriately.

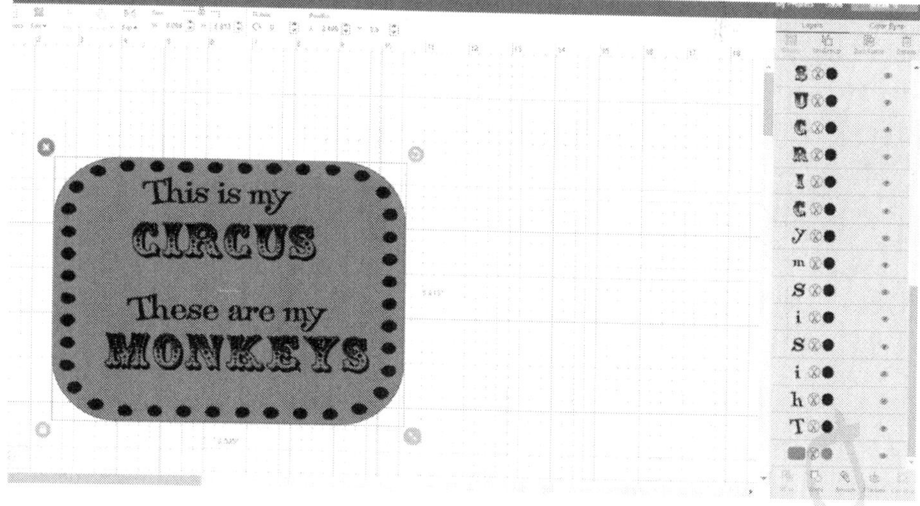

If you attach this now it will attach all of them and turn everything the same color. You probably don't want to do this. The next best thing is to attach the black dot frame and the words.

First you will want to detach the attachment you just made, and now I will show you how to do finish this project!

Select just the purple frame and grab it and pull it aside. This will leave you with just the frame and the letters.

Select "attach" and this will now attach the black dot frame and the letters!
You can now drag and pull the black frame back onto the rounded purple box.

Once you're happy with your placement, you can go ahead and push the cut or "make it" button. Now that you've pushed it, try not to panic. You will see a whole new screen. It will tell you to prepare two mats, but you can get away with just using one if that's all that you have.

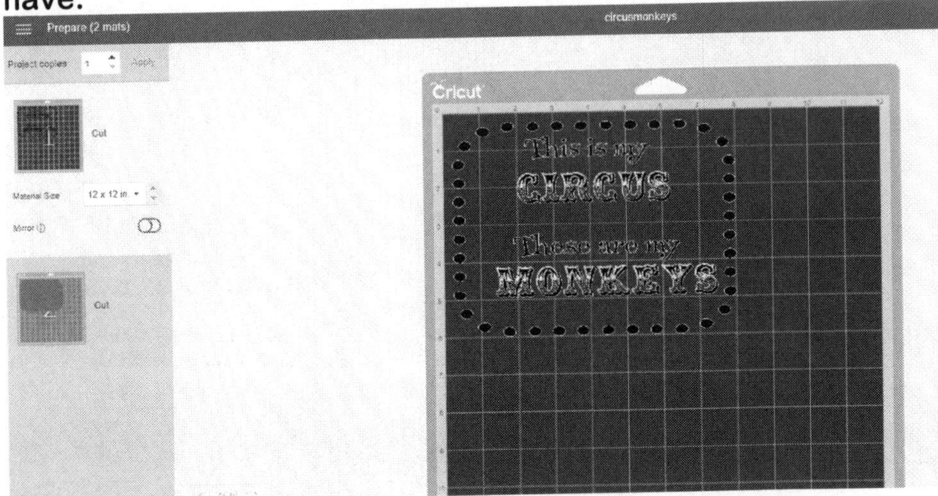

First up, we have project copies. How many of these are you wanting to make? Do you want to print multiple copies of this, or do you want to do just one?
For now, let's just stick with one.
Then going down the line, we have the different colors of the different layers of this design. You can click on them to see where they are going to lay out on the cutting mat. (Also, if I were cutting this out with heat transfer vinyl, I would want to make sure the "Mirror Image" option was checked on all the mat layouts, otherwise, this would probably end in disaster, and would not look right. I've done this too many times to count!)
Also on this, you can change where the items will be on the cutting mat. To do so, simply pick the layer that you want to change, and click and drag the items around. Once you are satisfied, you can hit the "Continue" button in the lower right-hand corner.

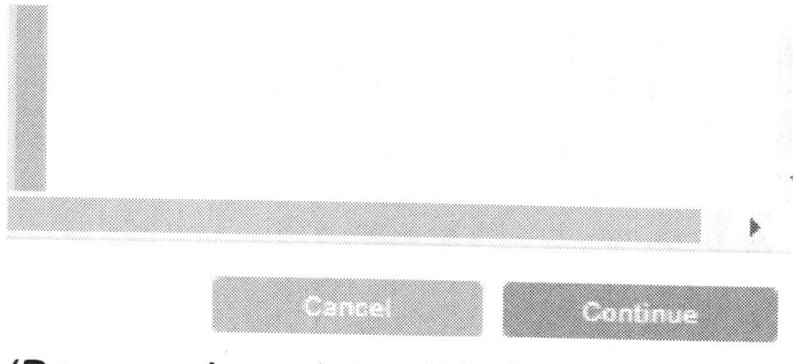

(Because I am doing this for demonstration purposes, I won't be using HTV, and instead will be using regular vinyl. HTV is very expensive, and vinyl will still demonstrate without the waste of the HTV. At this point, you will want to double-check everything. Make sure that you have clicked the iron button for iron on material, and make sure that you have everything situated where you want it to be. If using HTV you will need to make sure it is mirrored to get the effect that you want when you apply the vinyl to material. You are about to reach the point of no return! If you've hit go, you can still cancel the cut!) Uh oh! You've made a mistake. What now?! In the upper right-hand corner, there will be an X. Click this. The machine will ask if you want to cancel the cut, select yes.

I will use purple and black vinyl to use for this demonstration.
I have my two colors of vinyl now, so I am ready to cut my first one:
I will hit the Go button and then get the screen above. I want to make sure that I am using the correct dial setting so this is where I will check to make sure that I have that setting on "vinyl."

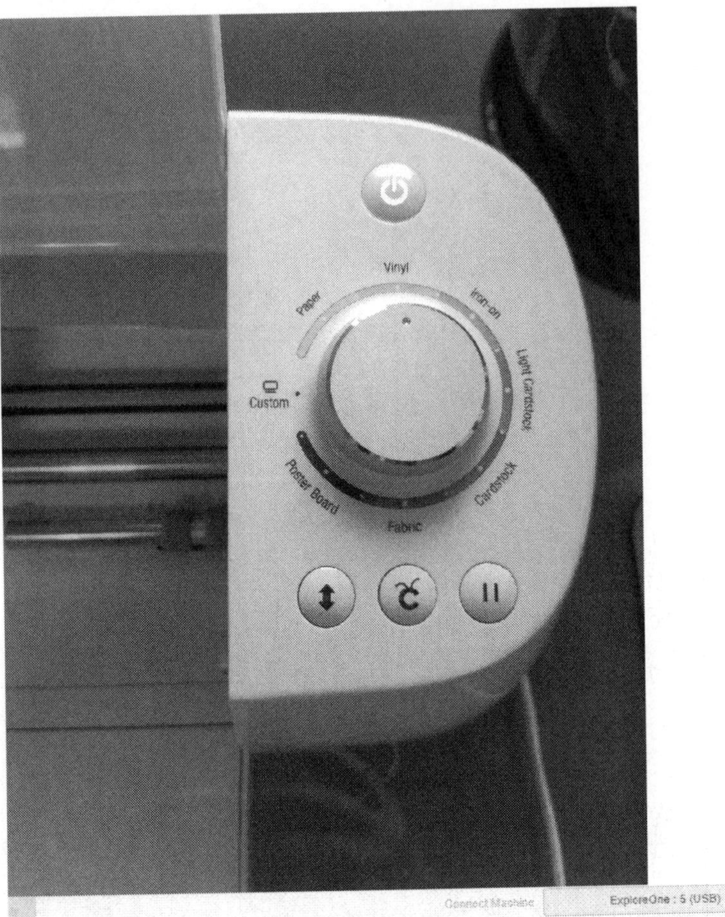

Connect Machine ExploreOne : 5 (USB)

① Material set to: Vinyl

Adjust dial to desired material

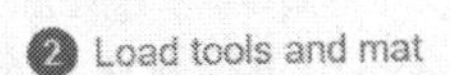

❷ Load tools and mat

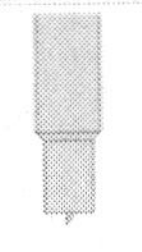

Load Fine-Point Blade in Clamp ⓘ

Choose Another Blade

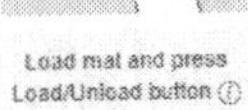

Load mat and press Load/Unload button ⓘ

③ Press Go

Next, I will load the mat. I first put my vinyl on, make sure it is pressed down firm, but not too firmly, and then place the mat into the machine. Note that I do not use a full sheet of vinyl; only what I will need for the project. To do this, line up your cutting mat with the bars, and hit the blinking white arrow.

Once the machine registers, it will ask you to hit the cut button which is the C with the antenna on it.

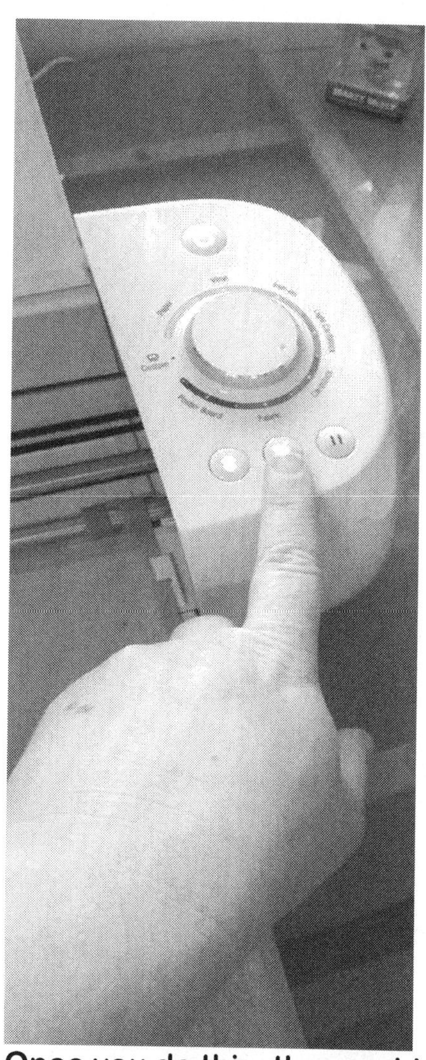

Once you do this, the machine will start cutting.
(If you see it start to tear or rip the material, hit the pause button and unload the mat. This will stop the cut and will stop you from wasting material.)
When you are done, you will hit the load button again, and this will release your mat. You will add another piece of vinyl load it into the machine and hit the cut button again. You will do this until you are done, and then you will hit the finish button on the computer screen once complete. You can see your progress on the cutting page, and it will look like this:

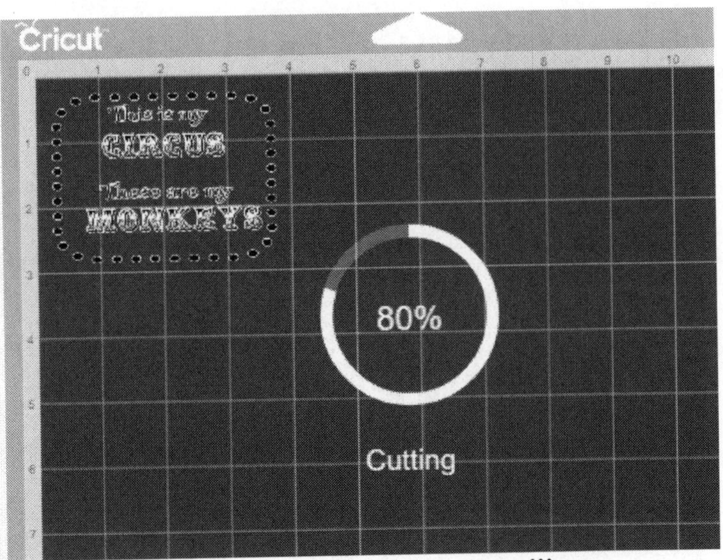

When you are done, in the bottom right, you will see "Finish." Hit this button and it will take you back to the main screen.

Now you have your cut materials. You may have had difficulty getting them off the mat and this is where your spatula and weeding tools can come in handy!

Once you have lifted the pieces all up, you can then piece your design together. (You can use glue of your preference including hot glue, super glue, tacky glue, or Mod Podge if you prefer.)

And there! You have completed your first Cricut Cut!

Now you can do anything you can imagine with this.

I do, want to go back and talk about Custom Settings though for just a minute. I know you probably noticed a custom setting on your dial, so let's look at this for just a minute. The custom setting is where you can select from a variety of materials to cut with. Cricut lists the most commonly used items on the main dial, but the custom dial is where you can set the machine to cut nearly anything.

Walk with me through this and turn your dial to Custom on your machine.

Once you select this option, the following screen will pop up allowing you to custom set material.

View All will allow you to view the different types of materials that the Cricut can cut.

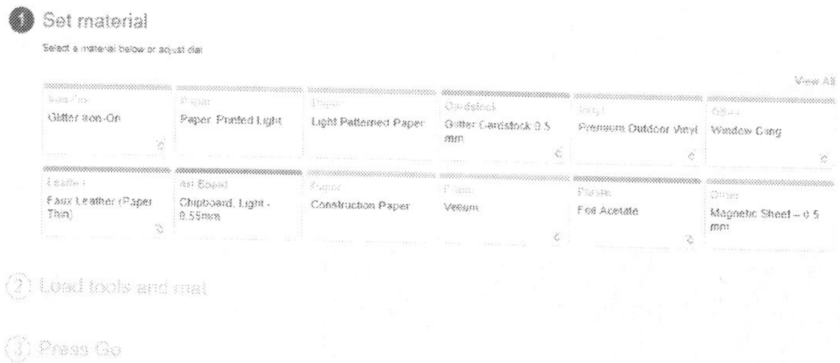

1 Set material

Select a material below or adjust dial

View All

Glitter Iron-On
Paper, Printed Light
Light Patterned Paper
Glitter Cardstock 0.5 mm
Premium Outdoor Vinyl
Window Cling
Faux Leather (Paper Thin)
Chipboard, Light - 0.55mm
Construction Paper
Vellum
Foil Acetate
Magnetic Sheet – 0.5 mm

2 Load tools and mat

3 Press Go

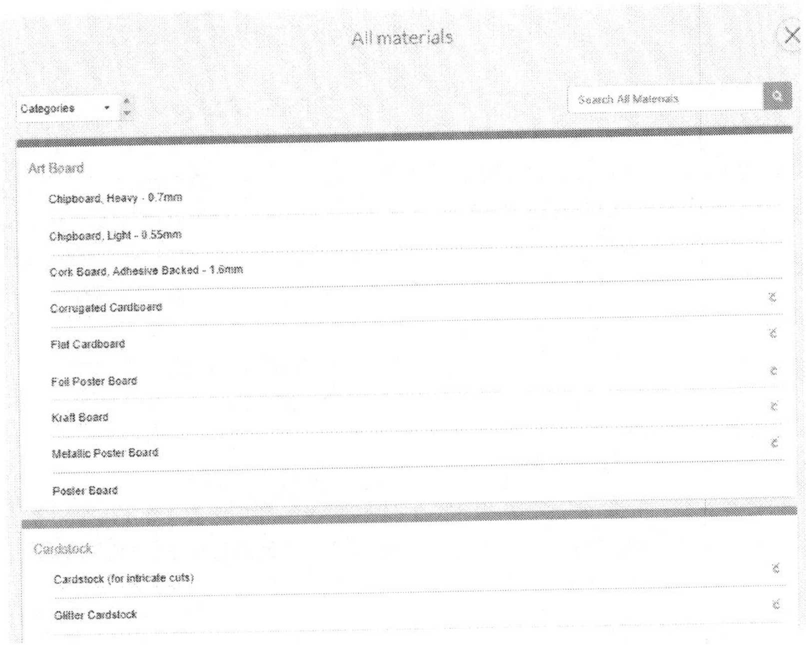

All materials

Categories

Search All Materials

Art Board

Chipboard, Heavy - 0.7mm

Chipboard, Light - 0.55mm

Cork Board, Adhesive Backed - 1.6mm

Corrugated Cardboard

Flat Cardboard

Foil Poster Board

Kraft Board

Metallic Poster Board

Poster Board

Cardstock

Cardstock (for intricate cuts)

Glitter Cardstock

And here you can find just about any other type of material that you would want to use to cut with. Sometimes (and we'll talk about this more in the troubleshooting chapter) you will find that the Cricut standard settings don't work for the vinyl or cardstock you are cutting. You can come here to the Custom settings, and try something else out that may work a bit better for you! Otherwise, if you have some odd material that you want to cut that may not fit the normal mode, you will find it here in the custom settings option.

End of Chapter Author's Note

As you explore (no pun intended) your machine and how to use it, you will get more familiar with some of the various steps and how-tos. There are many other tutorials available for advanced work with your Cricut on the web including YouTube and many blog sites. I encourage you to get comfortable with the basics first, and then move on to more advanced techniques and usages of the machine. It can be a bit intimidating, and you want to make sure you are comfortable prior to starting more advanced uses of the machine to prevent frustration.

Later, in this book, I will walk you through two projects that you can try yourself to get a bit more experience. One will be with vinyl and a tumbler and the other will be using cardstock.

Chapter 5

Uh Oh! Troubleshooting

Earlier in this book, I mentioned that Design Space is not without its flaws, and this is where we will get into some of that nitty gritty. For a web based software, it's not bad, but it does occasionally glitch. It is my opinion that Cricut/ProvoCraft does not have the hosting capacity for the number of users that use its software program and this is probably what causes most glitches. I believe that if they offered an offline software that people could download, most of the glitches that users experience would nearly disappear. Again, this is just my opinion, but there are problems occasionally.

Sometimes errors occur because of the web browser you are using. Always make sure your web browser is up to date. Also, don't use Internet Explorer if you can help it. Not only is it not really supported anymore, it doesn't work as well as Chrome or Firefox.

First up, common problems:

Is your machine turned on?

Is your machine plugged into your computer?

Believe it or not, these are the two most common problems newbies experience. It's ok, we've all been there. Just plug it in and hopefully you will be on your merry way.

My machine is making a funny grinding noise!

If this happens, you will need to reach out to Cricut. Usually this is because the machine needs to be oiled, and Cricut will send you the special oil to oil up your machine. In most cases, this appears to take care of the problem.

ERROR: Shockwave Plugin Has Crashed

ERROR: Please remove exclusive content.

ERROR: Shockwave plugin is not responding.

ERROR: Unknown Error

Thankfully, these errors seem to have been eradicated with the new Design Space. Previously design space operated using Adobe Flash, and there were constant errors. Since the new Design Space, this appears to have been completed eliminated!

ERROR: Image is too large for a cutting mat. Please reduce the Image size.

This depends on what you are trying to cut. If you are trying to cut a 6 foot by 6-foot banner, forget about it. Otherwise, if you are making a sign, you may need to splice the images and reconnect them later and make them appropriate to the cutting mat that you are using. Use your rulers as your guide for this, and measure twice, cut once. (Keep in mind that this is a more advanced option for Cricut crafting, so you should be familiar with doing this prior to kicking off a 3-foot large customized character.)

Error: Your Cricut Machine is in Use- Reset

Your computer may be doing updates. Simply wait for these to finish and this error message should clear right up.

ERROR: Check your Internet Connection

Are you connected to the web? Check this, and you may need to reset your router again as well.

ERROR: Characters not supported

Sometimes this will happen if an SVG file is not formatted correctly. Reformat the SVG and try again. You may also want to reach out to the creator of the SVG. Sometimes you can also try logging out and logging back in again and it will load. This may also happen with JPEG and PNG image uploads as well. Occasionally this will also happen with various fonts. Some are simply not Cricut friendly and will not work in Design Space. In that case, you can turn it into an image and upload it, and it should work for you.

These are just a few of the more common errors that you may experience when using your Cricut. You can also visit the Cricut website to learn more at http://help.cricut.com/ or chat or call them:

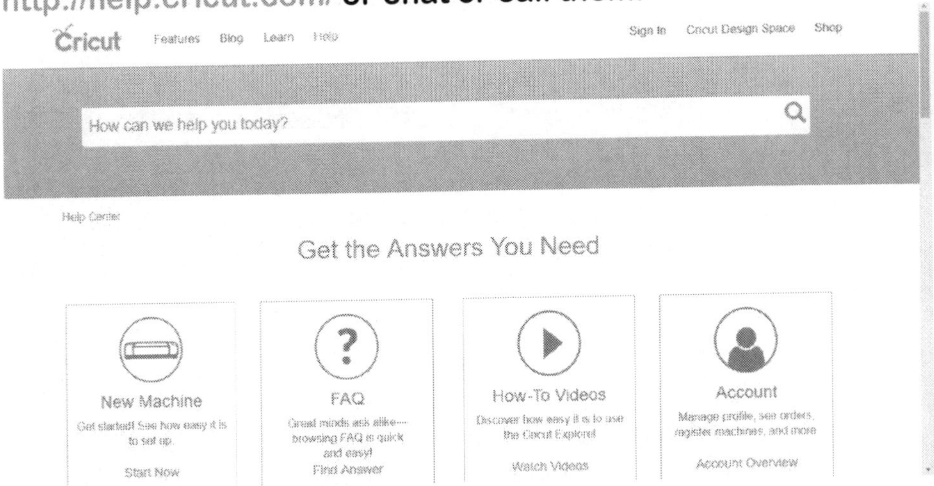

Chapter 6

Machine and Tool Maintenance

You've spent a lot of money and investments in your machine, so you want to make sure that it stays clean and useful for a long time to come. If you don't already have one, I recommend a dustcover. I made one for my Cricut and then created a pattern that I sell on Etsy for it. I have a toddler and critters, so I wanted to protect my machine. I chose duck cloth for the material to cover it with, but you can choose what you need to for your own machine. You can purchase these online as well, but at any rate, I recommend having one.

Let's talk about cleaning your machine. Believe it or not, baby wipes are one of the most useful items that I have found for cleaning my Cricut machine. They are cheap, and they can get the crud off a rusted bumper, without causing damage to the machine itself. You can use this to wipe down the machine and to get rid of some of the buildup.

As I mentioned earlier, you'll want to make sure to have a sharp blade. For most projects that experience trouble in the cutting stage, it is due to a dull blade. You can sharpen your blades by poking them into an aluminum foil ball a few times. When a blade gets too old, throw it into a Sharps container to get rid of it. (Please don't throw these in the trash.)

You will want to keep your mats clean and protected as well. Don't throw away the plastic film that comes with them- reuse this to keep the mat clean and protected. In Chapter 3 I talk about how to keep them clean. Other suggestions for this include baby wipes, lint roller brushes, and scraping tools. You will find what works best for you.

If you use scissors, pick a pair that you will have and use ONLY for your crafting projects. They will become dull, and if your house becomes anything like mine, you will constantly be yelling about someone "stealing" your scissors. Hide them and put them away and only use them for your crafts.

Keep your cords put away and not plugged in when not in use. This can help prevent fraying of the power and USB cords so that you don't end up with a Cricut that can't power on or connect to your computer. Replacement cords are available, but they are expensive.

You will want to keep your materials clean. Overtime, they will get worn out and you will need to replace them, but if you take care of them from the beginning, they should last you a long time.

Chapter 7

Supplies (aka Becoming a Craft Hoarder)

One of the most commonly asked questions is where to get supplies. My answer to this is that it depends on what you want to do! There are tons of supply options and what you use will depend on what you plan to do with your items and what you hope to accomplish.

The first place to start is your local dollar store. Here you can get tumblers, coffee mugs, plates, scrapers, towels, baskets, and more for just a buck. Want to work with vinyl, but need some practice first? Start here, you won't regret it. Of, if you live in an area that doesn't have a dollar store, there is always http://www.dollartree.com/ where you can order supplies to be dropped shipped right to you.

Let's start with the basics. Cardstock. Usually you can't go wrong with Michaels, JoAnn, or Hobby Lobby. These stores often run 50-60% off sales and you can get cardstock dirt cheap. You will find yourself buying stuff even when you don't always need it! This can get expensive, so try to keep track of your inventory. You can also sign up to be a preferred member and get coupons at each of these stores, and they are worth it, totally and completely. (Cricut has cardstock too, but is often quite expensive compared to the craft stores that also sell it.)

Next up and the next most popular supplies tend to be vinyl. Vinyl can be complicated, so let's run through the basics quickly. First, there is removable vinyl. This is often referred to as Oracal 631 or repositionable vinyl. Secondly, there is permanent vinyl, or Oracal 651. Next, you have "heat transfer vinyl." AKA HTV. If you are using fabric of any kind, you want to use HTV. You cannot use regular vinyl to make shirts. They won't stick, and you will ruin your clothing materials, iron, ironing board or heat press, and stink up the place. Just don't do it. Trust me.

My favorite and preferred place to get vinyl is VinylWorld651. http://vinylworld651.com/ They have super-fast shipping, the owner is awesome to work with, and they happen to have a location 20 minutes from my house. I cannot recommend them enough. (Disclaimer: I receive no kickbacks or incentives from VinylWorld 651, I just recommend them due to the great customer service that I have personally received from them. They are also local to me, and I can go pick up vinyl any time that I need it.) They offer so many different types of vinyl as well as supplies that they can ship directly to you. Check them out- you won't be disappointed, and they often run sales.

You are certainly welcome to find your own vinyl supplier, and check out what is available to you on the web!

I recommend if you are using HTV that you obtain a heat press. Irons just do not cut it when it comes to making and creating things to sell. I say this personally and professionally. There are many types of heat presses available, but let me say this: if the deal seems too good to be true, it is. There are heat press scams all over the internet and often people are left with nothing but a financial loss. You can find used ones on Craigslist and yard sale sites occasionally.

Cricut also offers a type of heat press now. It is called the Cricut Easy Press. It runs around $149.99, and you can occasionally catch it on sale. Cricut claims that it works in 60 seconds or less and that it works with all types of HTV that are available. At this point it is still too new to offer any type of feedback, but so far, the responses to it have been positive. The biggest complaint is that it is not quite large enough to handle bigger projects.

Along with the heat press, you probably want to use shirts and other materials. You can start with your local Michaels or Joann's. They often run t-shirt deals 5 for $10.00. For $2.00 a piece, you can't go wrong.

If you want to buy t-shirts in bulk, visit Jiffy Shirts. http://www.jiffyshirts.com/ They have hundreds of t-shirts available and you can buy them in bulk. They ship fast, and you can even get discounts as a repeat customer. You can also find many types and variety of shirts such as long sleeve, baseball, sweatshirt, etc.

If you are wanting to buy bulk cups, tumblers, and other items, I can recommend Save A Cup. https://www.saveacup.com/ Many varieties and different types of items are available on this site, and they have fast shipping. You can also try your local Dollar Tree or Dollar Store.

As far as other types of “blanks” go, just be careful who you choose. There are several available if you go to Google and type in “blanks” and search around for what you are looking for. You can also join various Facebook groups that offer blanks as well. Some prefer to order from AliExpress, but this is an overseas shipper, and you may or may not get your items. Buyer beware.

Need wood and other supplies? Visit Lowes or Home Depot. They will slice, dice, and carry the stuff to the car for you at a cheap and affordable price. You can get all sorts of stuff at these home goods stores, and they may even have a scrap pile they will let you dig through at no additional change.

Another great place to keep your eyes on for reclaimed items is on Craigslist and Garage Sale sites. Look for free wood, pallet wood, free tile, etc. and you can easily clean up a garage worth of goodies in no time.

Once you get familiar with using your machine and what you need, the sky is the limit. Keep in mind that it is addictive, and you will end up with more than you need. I have totes and tubs of items sitting around waiting to be used, and I am embarrassed by this. When you are getting started, try to purchase only what you need, and then go from there. If there is a deal that is too good to pass it, pounce on it, but try to not go after more than you need!

Chapter 8

I want to run my own business!

To begin this chapter, let me first start off by saying, I am not a lawyer. I am a nurse by trade, and though I hold a doctoral degree, it is not in law. With that said, I am going to share with you what I have learned about starting a small business and the tips and tricks that come with that. Let me repeat; I am not a lawyer. You may wish to consult with a lawyer prior to opening your business. There are affordable websites for this, or you may know someone who is a lawyer and can help you with getting started. Some may even offer free consultations.

What's in a Name?

Your small business name is probably what is going to attract new visitors right away. I chose Mon Amie Creations for my small business. It is a play-off of my name, and it's fun. My logo includes my name and a small design. This is what people will recognize as me and my "brand." Pick something that you will want to have long term; especially if you are registering everything. You don't want something hip for the time being and then be sick of it after 6 months because by then you'll have to go through a lot of trouble to change your name.

Choose a reputable designer. Don't use something like Fiverr where you get stuck with something that you may not love. Etsy has some great designers, or feel free to reach out- I am happy to see what I can come up with for you!

What Makes Me Stand Out?

What do you plan to make or create that will allow you to stand out from the competition? If you plan to sell on Etsy, or one of the many self-selling sites, you will find hundreds of variations of the same projects and products.

Come up with something new, creative, innovative, and something original. Try to not be like everyone else. On top of that it allows you to avoid potential copyright and trademark law by creating something of your own design.

You can also sell on local Mom sites, local yard sale sites, Facebook Marketplace, and even site such as OfferUp, and other apps. I have tried them all and have varying degrees of success with them all.

Business Registration

You may or you may not want to register your business. There are pros and cons to each, and therefore speaking with a lawyer is important. If you are wanting to do this, and do in in package form, you may want to check out a company such as Legal Zoom who simplifies and does all the work and registering for you. https://www.legalzoom.com/. They can also help you decide if registering just a DBA, LLC, or Incorporating is your best choice. I personally use a DBA and file taxes as an individual, but you may wish to do something different. Some prefer to keep their personal and professional lives separate, and that is perfectly fine. Either way, you will want to consider what your local laws are as well. Research Federal, State, and Local to make sure you comply. A company like Legal Zoom can help with this.

Accounting

You need to do accounting to keep track of where your money comes and goes. Companies that offer self-selling services like Etsy provide you with annual statements and you can download everything into neat Excel spreadsheets. This is helpful for keeping track of all accounting purposes and where your money is going. Etsy of course takes their share, so be considerate of this.

You may want to consider account software such as QuickBooks or something similar. QuickBooks can be expensive and if you do a quick Google search, you can find several free options to get you started.

Payments

How will your customers pay you? This is something else to consider as you are working maybe at a craft show, or offline. There are many payment options that are available including the old-fashioned cash or check, but you can also use PayPal, Square, Swipe, and even Etsy Instant Sell. There are many options, but you will need to choose the best one for you.

Also, don't do ANY work without getting payment first! I can't stress this enough. Otherwise you will be left with customized products, no payment, and no customer. I have seen this happen too many times, and I personally insist on payment upfront and first. (And treat family members the way you would any other customer!)

Marketing

Marketing this day and age is not too difficult. You can create a Facebook page, get free business cards, and use word of mouth to get the message out about your new business. You can also sell at local craft shows, donate items for special auctions (if they agree to let you advertise your business) and work with companies to sell your designs and creations.

End of Chapter Author's Note:

Running a business is hard work. I do my crafting casually and only do very small amounts of paid work. It is fun and rewarding, but you need to make sure you are doing it for the right reasons and that you are jumping into this with your eyes wide open.

You will also need to invest time and money up front, and don't expect to have customers right away. It may take up to a year before you are making good money.

Everyone wants to work from home or make it big, but the reality is, is that you need to have a niche and a niche market to be successful.

Chapter 9

Recommended Resources

Note: I receive no kickbacks and have no conflicts of interest from the recommendations that I am providing. I have simply used and utilized these resources before and can personally recommend them.

Free SVG Sites:
LoveSVG http://www.lovesvg.com/%20
Facebook Groups
TheHungryJpeg http://www.thehungryjpeg.com
Cricut https://home.cricut.com/free-images
Vinyl:
VinylWorld651 http://www.vinylworld651.com
Cardstock:
Michaels
JoAnn's
Hobby Lobby
Business Registration:
Legal Zoom http://www.legalzoom.com
Free Font Sites:
http://www.dafont.com
http://www.thehungryjpeg.com
https://www.fontsquirrel.com/
http://www.1001freefonts.com/
http://www.fontspace.com/
https://www.urbanfonts.com/
Free Design Programs:
http://www.inkscape.org
T-Shirt Ordering:
Jiffy Shirts http://www.jiffyshirts.com/

You can also check Michaels and Joann's for sales.

<u>Blank Tumblers, Cups, and Mugs:</u>

SaveACup http://www.saveacup.com

Dollar Tree http://www.dollartree.com

<u>Wood and Tile Supplies:</u>

Lowes

Home Depot

Chapter 10

2 Free Project Ideas

Project One
Vinyl Coffee Mug

Items Needed:
Blank Coffee Mug
2 Colors of permanent vinyl
Cutting Mat
Cricut Machine
Weeding Tools
Transfer Paper
Squeegee
Alcohol and Alcohol Wipes

First make sure you prep your mug. You will want to wash it with soap and water and once dry, wipe it down with alcohol. This will ensure that the vinyl will stick when it's applied.
Upload your SVG files that you wish to use into Design Space.

Once uploaded into Design Space, you will want to resize the image until it is about 3 inches by 3 inches or so. (Or however large you would like it to be. The larger it is though, the harder it will be to transfer.) Keep in mind that you want it to fit on the cup. Perhaps you have one of those giant cups- by all means, resize it to 6x6 to get it to show up!
Now you are ready to make your item. Hit the “Make It” button at the top right of the screen.
This project will take one to two sheets of vinyl. If you have two mats, then prepare one with one color, and one with the other color. If not, just one the one mat, and add a color.
Place your Cricut to “Vinyl” for the cutting, and select “Go” in the bottom right.
Place your first sheet of vinyl on the mat
Load your mat.
Select the Cut button. (The C with antenna on the machine.)
Unload the mat.
Load the next mat with vinyl and load the mat into the machine.
Select the Cut button.
Unload the mat, and select the Finish button on the bottom of your screen.
You are done with the computer, so put this aside.
You now have two sheets of vinyl that you will need to “weed.” Weeding is the processing removing unwanted areas so that you see only want you want to see. I also recommend cutting away excess vinyl to save or re-use.

Once you have weeded these areas you will have two areas that you will need to transfer. We will transfer the pink square first. Take your transfer paper and place it over top of the vinyl is still attached to the white paper. Rub your squeegee over this. Lift gently. Place the transfer paper and vinyl onto your coffee mug. Make sure it is squared up and straight. Rub the transfer paper and vinyl onto the mug. You can also use the squeegee to make sure that it is completely attached. Remove the contact paper.
Complete the same steps for the black writing. Only this time, you will place the black writing directly onto the pink square. Squeegee this with the contact paper still attached.
Carefully remove the contact paper. If you find that areas are still sticking, leave the contact paper on, squeegee some more, and lift a little more.
Once you have done this, allow the coffee mug to "cure" or sit for about 24 hours prior to using or handwashing. And now you've completed your first easy vinyl project! Congratulations!

Project 2
Items needed
Cutting mat
Cricut Machine
Weeding Tools
Spatula
2 Pieces of Cardstock
Craft Glue
For this project, we will create a card that can be found in the Cricut Access Freebies. To begin, visit https://us.cricut.com/design/ and "Create New Project." Select insert images in the upper left:

Next, you will want to search for a card to cut. Visit the search bar. Near this you will see a funny looking funnel; click on this.

When you open this, select "free." (Note: this is also where you can view your cartridges as well.)

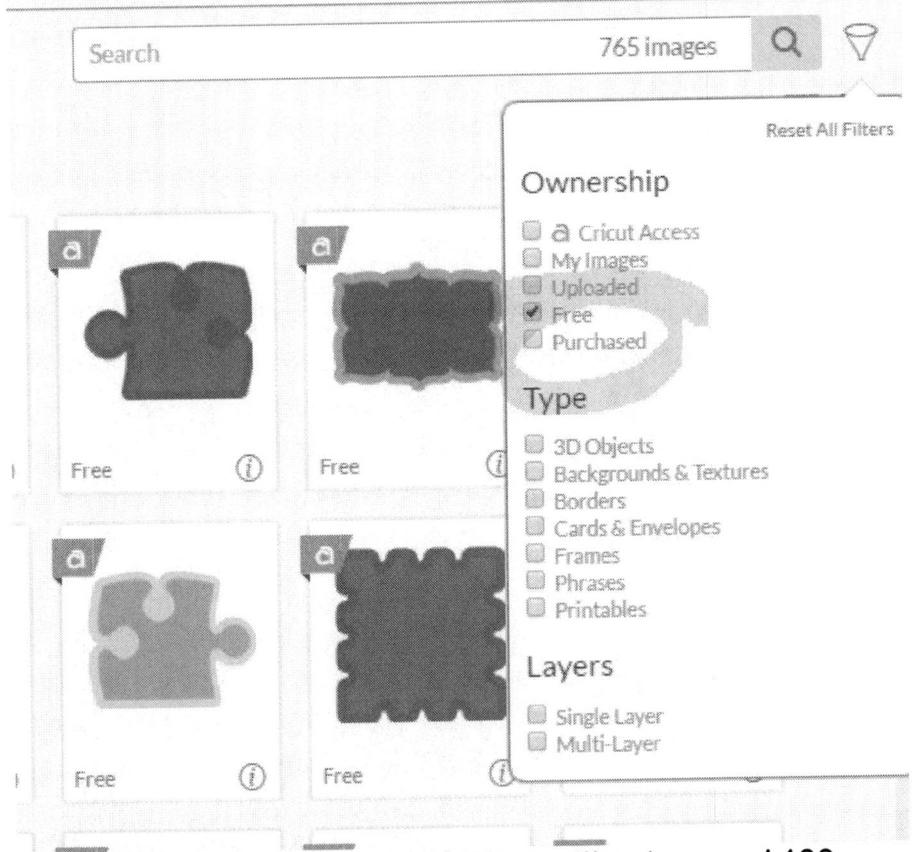

In the search bar, type "Card." You will get around 100 responses or so.
Select this card:

And then select “insert image” in the lower left-hand side:

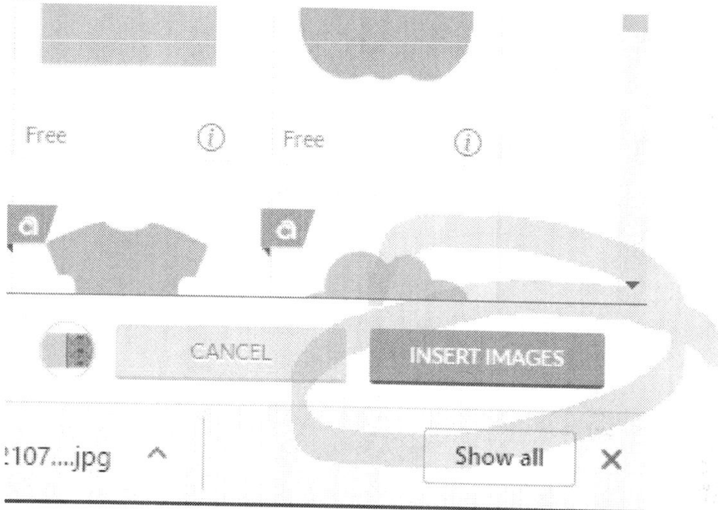

And now this card will be loaded into your design space. For this project, you can also add a piece of white card stock and write on the card, but we will just be cutting the card out for this exercise.
Resize the image to about 7.5 x 5 inches or so.
Select the Go button.
Place your first piece of cardstock on the mat.
Load the mat.
Turn the dial to Cardstock.
Select Cut.
Unload the mat, and reload with a new piece of cardstock.

Select Cut.
Unload the mat, and select finish.
You will want to use your spatula and weeding tools to remove the top part of the card. Do this carefully as they can easily tear.
Once both pieces are removed, you can glue them together with craft glue, and now you have created your first card!

Made in the USA
Lexington, KY
21 June 2018